Discovering Your Psychic Self

Edward Gordon

BLACK SPIRIT PUBLISHING

Black Spirit Publishing
P.O. Box 2428, PMB# 8443
Pensacola, FL 32513

ISBN 978-0-9838971-7-0

First Edition

For rights information, contact Black Spirit Publishing by mail or e-mail:

10 9 8 7 6 5 4 3 2 1

For Melody,
Who has always been there.

Table of Contents

Sagittarius is the astrological constellation of the 9th house. It stands for philosophy, religion, higher learning, travel, and curiosity. So, let us let Sagittarius lead us through pages of this book.

Introduction

The purpose of *Discovering Your Psychic Self* is to provide the knowledge, practices, and direction necessary to become a psychic person and live life at its highest level. It is intended to produce psychic self-realization and enlightenment.

Unit One covers the basic knowledge needed to realize your psychic nature. It examines what you really are, the true nature of God, and the true existence of your mind apart from your brain.

Unit Two explores the basic psychic practices of centering, grounding, and shielding yourself from negative influences. You will learn why each one is important, and how to easily achieve it.

Finally, Unit Three probes the psychic arts, because practicing a psychic art is what strengthens the parapsychological aspects of our mind, and that is the mental strength you need to discover our psychic self.

I base the information in this book on my decades of study in spirituality, psychism, religion, and the occult. Some of that study occurred in college; some was gained experientially as a professional psychic, and some came through suffering a great deal of trial and error.

But whatever the delivery mechanism, the wisdom I've gained has helped me live my life at its highest psychic potential. I hope sharing this wisdom results in the same for you.

—Edward Gordon, 2017

Unit One

Essential Psychic Knowledge

———————— • ————————

This unit must come first. It contains essential knowledge you must acquire before beginning the practice of the core psychic skills or setting out to discover what your psychic art should be.

We'll look at three key areas that relate to spirituality and psychic development: You, God, and the Mind. We'll see that you are not what you think you are, God is not what we think he is, and the mind is a whole lot more than the common notions we have of it.

This section may be deep at times, but you'll have no problem comprehending it, and you may find it gives you a brand-new perspective on the things that matter most.

Chapter 1

What Are You?

——————•—————

If we are going to embark on a journey toward psychic self-realization and enlightenment, and that is the goal of this book, we must talk first about *you*—the definition of you. Unless you know what you truly are, there's no way to improve psychically, because to improve psychically, the number one rule is to face the truth in all things, and that truth starts with the truth about you.

You'll notice I didn't say we're going to look at *who* you are. That's what so many spiritual self-help and psychology self-help books try to accomplish. They try to get you to know who you are. They never realize the impossibility of that task, owing to its prematurity. You can't know *who* you are until you know *what* you are. Besides, coming to know who you are, in your entirety, is what the whole of existence is about. You won't learn that much in this book, or even in your lifetime. *Who* you are is a mystery that your eternal soul came into existence to figure out—and even more *to create* as you go along throughout the vast expanse of time.

So, I can't tell you who you are, but if I can tell you what you are, perhaps that will set you on a better course for exploring the vastness of who you are. Maybe what you learn in this single book will stick with you throughout your many lifetimes and incarnations to come, and with a firm grasp of what you are in mind, *who* you are will become easier to figure out. That's the goal anyway.

So, with that said, to start the work of understanding what you are, you must understand the three "yous" that make up a human being. All human beings, including you, have these three aspects to their nature. The physical you, the astrological you, and the psychic you. The idea is to get your mind wrapped around the psychic self, because that's the full understanding of what you are. Sadly, few ever get passed the physical self, so let's start with that.

The Physical You

You probably know someone like Janet. Janet is overweight. When she was a teenager, she was only slightly overweight, and this gave her a buxom figure that had lots of young men wanting to get to know her better. But as she grew older, sadly, she grew bigger, and today she is seriously obese.

She tries to dress for it; her actual wardrobe is mostly oversized clothes, and she notices a lot of other women at work, and a lot of the men as well, are bigger than she is. So, this gives her some solace. She can look at them and feel a little better about herself, but that fragile bit of self-esteem breaks with the first magazine cover in the check-out line at the grocery store.

Always smiling at her is some celebrity, beautiful and slim, so slim her entire number on the scale is only the amount that Janet is overweight. It only takes that one reminder to bring her back to the reality of her physical self. She feels ugly. She used to feel beautiful, and now she feels so unappealing she can hardly stand to think about it. Every diet has failed, and she's given up hope of every regaining what she once had. To her, she is what she sees in the mirror.

But it gets worse. Her doctor recently told her that she's diabetic. She's developed type II diabetes in the last year or so, and most assuredly because of her weight. The doctor has prescribed insulin. She is to start checking her blood sugar three times a day. She's always hated shots, but now she has to give them to herself every day, and prick her finger with a needle three times a day! A depression sets in, and that's when the voices start.

She's not crazy, and she doesn't think she is, but every time she checks her blood sugar, each time she pricks her fingertip with the lancet, it's like something or someone she doesn't know in her mind starts telling her how fat she is. It tells her that she's disgusting, that she deserves her disease. It's a malicious voice, and it's growing stronger. Consequently, she's stopped checking her blood sugar. She tries to ignore her situation the best she can. She feels like that's her only option.

But Janet's problem is not her weight. Her problem is an illusion she keeps. The demon that torments her has not come to her because she packed on some pounds after high school. It's come to her because of the lie she believes.

She fantasizes and honestly believes that if she could just stick to a diet, get the gastric bypass her doctor talked about, lose the weight, get back to a size eight, if she could just do that, then her problems would be solved. That's all she thinks about, but it's a lie.

Janet's problem is that she doesn't know *what* she is. She thinks she's the person in the mirror, and accepting that definition of herself as the truth has sabotaged her diets, her health, and invited the voices that bring her down.

What Janet needs to learn is a basic spiritual truth we all need to learn, even if you don't have Janet's problem, this is still the very first lesson you must learn in psychic training: *You are not your physical body.*

Sure, you use a physical body in the physical world, but as everyone is aware, the body grows into an adult and begins to grow old thereafter until it dies. Once the body dies, it decays until only a skeleton is left, and eventually the skeleton decays, too, and the body becomes part of the dirt of the earth once again. The body comes from the dirt of the earth; it eats other bodies, whether plant or animal; it grows for a time, lives for a time, and then returns to the dirt from whence it came. How could that possibly encapsulate the totality of you?

But there's even more transience to the body: It is, after all, part of *time*. It exists in a universe of time. That means it is always changing. The body you have today is not the same body you had as a child. You have grown many times the size you were as an infant. Most of the cells in your body have replaced themselves over time, and the experiences and memories you have at this moment were not there a moment ago. So, even if you consider yourself to be your physical body—what body are you talking about? Is our Janet the body she was, or is she the body she is?

People often pay lip service to the idea that they are not their body. They talk as if they know they are spirits in the material world, but they *live* as though the dirt making up their physical body is the most important thing there is—and how we live signifies what we honestly believe.

If this were not true, our Janet wouldn't suffer from low self-esteem, but she does. Most people are convinced that what they see in the mirror is the definition of what they are. They do not realize that the first psychic lesson of life is to overcome what seems so obvious. And again, that first psychic lesson is that we are not our bodies. We only use our bodies to transport our minds through the physical universe. Our minds are riding our bodies like horses.

The point being that when you realize you are not your body, you can then take the next step toward becoming your psychic self.

The psychic self is a state of mind wherein a person no longer considers themselves defined by the physical world. Instead, they see themselves primarily as a spirit, especially a spirit connected monistically to the Divine Creator. We'll talk more about that connection in the chapter about God.

Psychic-self is the opposite of physical-first. Right now, Janet is physical-first. Unfortunately, if she is like most people, she will spend her whole life being physical-first until the day she dies. And all the while, she will detest herself for not being physically what she wants to be and what others tell her she should be.

Ironically, if she were to understand what she really is, if she could develop such a psychic self-realization, she'd probably lose weight. Most of her reasons for overeating would simply disappear. In time, she might even have to make sure she eats enough. Spiritual people frequently lose the desire to eat a great deal. Many become vegetarians and vegans.

She wouldn't identify as her body, so her body wouldn't control her as it once did toward either fat or thin. She would be free of her body long before her physical death in this world, and she'd be happier for it.

And, of course, there are lots of people in Janet's circumstances. They come in all shapes and sizes. If it's not a weight problem, then it's some other physical issue. And if it's not something that can be seen in the mirror, then it's something that makes their life equally miserable: maybe an addiction, maybe relationship problems, or maybe the decline of their physical stamina or health. Any of these can cause one to focus on themselves as a physical entity rather than as a psychic being.

The Astrological You

Along the way, out of our physical-first mentality, we encounter another definition of what we are: the astrological self. This is more advanced. Some people, when they experience their astrological self, believe they have found a form of enlightenment. For me, it launched a lifelong interest in astrology. Both my horoscope, and the horoscopes of others, utterly fascinate me. And certainly, those who find the astrological-self have taken the next step toward a psychic self-realization.

The goal in this section is not to teach you astrology. We'll look more closely at astrology in a later chapter. The goal, right now, is for you to understand your unique place in the universe. For sure, this unique status is symbolized by an individual's horoscope, but the point is that the next step in spiritual development is to get to a full understanding of what it means to be one of a kind. That's the *astrological you.*

To get to what you really are, you must, at some point, be able to look at yourself and tell yourself, "There is no one else like me in the world."

And that's an easy statement to brush off, because we say it tritely to children all the time. Of course, we know that we are original, even without direct proof, because the idea that there are others out there who are identical to us is absurd. We know we are unique, but knowing it and believing it, enough to live as if it were true, are two different things.

An astrological horoscope displays this uniqueness. In my case, there are lots of Virgos in the world. However, there are less Virgos with Sagittarius as a rising sign. There are even less of that combination that has Neptune in Scorpio in the 12th house, and as I go through my entire horoscope, and as I come to realize how a horoscope is cast, I soon realize that no one has the same horoscope as me. The same goes for you. No one has your horoscope, either.

But it's even deeper than that. It's not that you are one of a kind now; It's that you're one of a kind eternally. No one has ever been like you in the history of the universe. They say the universe started in the Big Bang some 13.7 billion years ago; you have never existed in the universe until you existed now. You are not just any original; you're an *absolute* original.

And yet, it goes even deeper than that, because not only are you truly unique in the history of the universe, it also means that when you pass away, there will never be anything like you again. There never has been, never will be. And what's so important about understanding this concept of the astrological you is that it gives at least one reason, even if there is nothing about you as a physical being that you like, it gives you one indisputable reason for God to love you.

The Orange Grove Lesson

We are always told that God loves us, but so often when we only concentrate on being physical-first, we can't find a logical reason why that should be. And we are logical, rational minds. So, without a reason to believe, we typically lose faith. What we see in the physical world is that physical life comes and goes like weeds; there's nothing special about it at all, so why should God love us?

I remember, as a kid, living in Riverside, California and riding my bike through an orchard one day. I was raised in the Pentecostal Christian religion, so I believed in all its precepts wholeheartedly. God loved me, they said, and though I was a wicked sinner (presumably, even by the age of twelve), God sent his son to die on a cross to save me from my sin and take me to heaven after I died.

I was told this, and I believed it, until I took that bike ride, a bike ride I had taken a hundred times before. But this time, I had a revelation. I didn't realize it was a revelation then. I didn't realize God was trying to show me something, to teach me something (which I am now trying to teach you). I didn't realize it then, but nevertheless, that revelation stayed with me all my life.

There were all these trees full of ripe oranges, it was nearly time for the harvest. As I rode through, I thought about how many oranges were in the entire grove, and then I thought about how they all come and go every year. So, I wondered, what was one orange worth?

It seemed to me that one orange, by itself, was worth nothing. It grows; it's picked and torn apart; it's digested or decays, and then it's gone forever. How many oranges were in the grove? How many groves were in California? How many in the entire world?

Then I thought about all the people in the world, and how each one comes and goes just like an orange on a tree in an orchard. The orchard had been there for decades. Humans, we learned in church, had been around for 5,000 years (even though in school we learned modern humans had been around about 200,000 years). Whatever the case, on my bike ride, I began to feel sad, even melancholy, because if we are all just passing like worthless oranges, and we had been doing so for countless ages, how could God possibly care enough about any one of us to love us?

It wasn't until decades later, when I first studied my astrological chart that I came to understand at least one reason why God *must* love us: We are literally one of a kind, and we will never be duplicated. Even if God decided to end the universe, start it over, and re-create me, that would only be my "re-creation." It would never be me again. It would be like one of a type—whereas I am one of a kind; my astrological chart proves it.

Apparently, God values us the same way we value works of art. He loves us, because when we are gone, we are gone forever, and that is an eternal loss to him.

So, it only makes sense then that if God wants to keep you, he must prepare a place on the astral plane for you and save you after you die. He must continue your existence, or lose you forever. And if he planned to lose you, he never would have created you as a one-of-a-kind object in the universe to begin with. He created you that way, because he loves you. You are his one-of-a-kind star child.

And yet, there is even more to the definition of what you are than that. More than just a physical being on the planet, more than a star child in the universe, there is a psychic dimension to you.

The Psychic You

Later, we're going to discuss three basic psychic skills: centering, grounding, and shielding, but before we can do that, you must come to a third level of understanding about what you are.

Our Janet looks in the mirror, steps on the scale, puts on her clothes, and all the while she thinks that is who she really is. So, even if she does accept that she's an absolute original star child intended by God, and loved by God, she still believes she is her physical self. She still has a physical-first mentality.

Because of this, she sees failure and decline from the physical person she was in high school. She takes the guilt of that failure and decline onto herself, and it morphs into self-loathing. The self-loathing becomes a personal pain that she carries with her at all times. It might even spill over into hostility, jealousy, and the judgment of others. Even when she's not feeling bad, she's not actually happy.

And if she were to slim up, she would still never be what she was in high school. Time has aged her, and the experiences and mistakes she's dealt with have made her harder and wiser than she was as a teen, so she sees the world differently now than she did back then. Such wisdom is often valued in our society, but it does come expensively with the loss of innocence and any sense of adventure. Her teen years are gone; her appearance is gone, and her health is fading. This is the harvest she has reaped from her physical-first mentality.

However, there is a way out. She need only see the truth, and that truth is that she is not a physical body at all. She is a mind.

We are all minds. The "you" in any sentence is referring to a mind not a body. The person you see in the mirror reflects a body that is being perceived by a mind.

Light strikes your face, bounces to the mirror, bounces back to your eyes, stimulates your optic nerve, which carries a signal to the occipital lobe of your brain, which triggers millions of neurons—but all for what reason? For your mind (for *you*) to perceive the physical appearance of your body.

You are a mind, and your mind does not require your body to exist. It exists independently from your brain. (We'll discuss this in Chapter Three.) Your mind is your consciousness—and that's you. In the end, that's the only you that matters.

Physical-first people believe the brain makes the mind. When they point to their mind, they point to their head. This is because it has always been understood that if you destroy a person's head, they no longer appear conscious. But what does that really prove?

If the mind exists independently of the brain and uses the brain psychokinetically to interact with the body to participate in the physical universe, if you destroy the brain, the mind would still be there, but the body would go limp just the same. So, brain activity and mind may seem to go hand in hand, but there's really no reason to believe they do.

If Janet understood and believed she was a mind and not a body, she would have a psychic self-realization. Granted, it might seem unfortunate that she has to move around a body she doesn't like, but that body would no more be her than an old car I drive is me. And if she came to that awareness, what might eventually arise from that understanding?

There would be no more need for self-loathing. In fact, she might find that the things of her mind are vastly more interesting than anything she is doing in this world with her body. She may come to find that discovering what she really is and how deep she goes matters far more than how much she weighs. She might even discover that she loves herself.

And this self-love is not at all like narcissism. Narcissism is born from self-hate. It's a mentally ill reaction to the inability to accept the imperfections of one's self. Narcissists must always tear down others to feel better about themselves. They must always try to convince others that they are superior. But real self-love isn't like that.

Real self-love comes from knowing what you really are. It comes from the revelation that you are a psychic being, not a physical-first body. And when your mind comes to realize its predominance in existence, it naturally wants to know more about itself. It wants to take the spiritual journey into itself to find out how deep it goes. What the mind finds on that journey is amazing, and that amazement transforms into real self-love, a love that radiates out to others like a nurturing light.

If Janet had that, she'd never step on a scale again, not if she didn't want to anyway. She might even find that her physical appetites decrease and her need for grounding (which we'll talk about later) increases, so she might become more active through walking and exercise. Ironically, she might even lose the weight she has utterly stopped caring about. Such can be the results of a higher psychic life.

Chapter 2

Understanding God

———————— • ————————

The next two chapters of this book are going to get a little deep. They're going to be deep, because the knowledge they contain is necessary for digging into all the spiritual tools of psychic training, and when you think about it, that's the way all training goes: first one gets the knowledge, then one can apply that knowledge. These chapters are the background knowledge we need to apply ourselves in this life as self-realized psychic people.

So, we start with God, but God is a confounding topic. People can't even agree on what God is. If you went to any church on any given Sunday and polled the parishioners, you wouldn't find two definitions of God that were the same, because everyone has their own god. Everyone needs their own god.

Everyone fashions God into a convenient shape that makes sense to them, favors them, and philosophically fits into their pocket so they can carry him around wherever they go and pray to him whenever they want. And that's fine; everyone is entitled to their own god. But in this chapter, we're not going to talk about the lowercase "g" god. We're going to talk about the uppercase "G." That's the Divine. That's the one you must come to understand if you're going to grow spiritually.

Below are four axioms about God. An axiom is an idea that is assumed to be fundamentally true. It's a bedrock on which other truths are built, and that's exactly what we're going to do with the axioms below. Because when you understand these axioms about God, you will start to understand why all the psychic stuff matters so much, and why becoming a psychic person matters so much to you personally. So, consider these four axioms:

1. God is not consciousness.

Most people think of God as a conscious person. They believe he has a mind like theirs. He hears and considers the prayers they send. He has emotions like anger and love, just like they do, and he has a plan for the earth and its residents.

The problem with that kind of god is that he couldn't possibly create and sustain a universe. The mind they think he has would be so limited by circumstance and causality, that he couldn't possibly have the mental capacity to hold all that exists in existence at every given moment. His mind would be like our own. And we can't create a universe, much less be attuned to everything going on in it at the same time. Consciousness itself would be a fundamental restriction on universal attunement.

And yet, the Divine Creator God created every quark (a quark is the smallest part of an atom), and he structured the universe to create every galaxy (Galaxies are considered the largest objects in the universe.). He is the cause of everything, so he can't be motivated to anger or motivated by the actions of the inhabitants of the earth. That would be a lower-case god.

Of course, this is not a new idea. The Ancient Israelites understood it. The prophet Isaiah wrote: *"For my thoughts are not your thoughts, neither are your ways my ways, saith the Lord. For as the heavens are higher than the earth, so are my ways higher than your ways, and my thoughts higher than your thoughts."* (Isaiah 55:8-9)

The fact is, a mind that not only creates order out of chaos and sustains every particle in the universe in a kind of perfect order and harmony, cannot be like you and me. That is a mind that is completely inaccessible to ours—at least at our level here and now.

Think of the last time you had a dream. In that dream, there was a landscape, air, maybe water, buildings, and probably people. Imagine asking one of the people in the dream about the mind that's creating the dream. They wouldn't be able to answer you. It's not that they are stupid; it's that their mind is a lower order mind. The mind creating the dream is not the same mind or consciousness as they are.

We are God's creatures, but we can no more comprehend what he is than a person in a painting can comprehend the artist that made the painting. So, when you consider God, you must realize that God is not conscious the way that you are. He is beyond consciousness; he is great-er than consciousness. And this is very important to un-derstand when we talk later about centering.

Changing our mind about God, and realizing he's a lot greater than our personal gods, is the intended effect of the first axiom, but this leads us necessarily to the second.

2. God exists and does not exist.

The atheists are right: there is no God. But that's not the whole story.

Back in in 1994, I bought a computer and went online for the first time. I think my browser was called Netscape, and the internet service was called Prodigy. If I remember correctly, you paid by the hour for access, so you only logged on and off when you had to.

The very first form of social networking, in those days, came in the form of newsgroups, and they were a cross between e-mail and a web forum. Someone would post a topic, and other people would respond to it. Your browser had an app called a newsreader, and the groups were called alt.this or alt.that. You could log on, download your newsgroup using the newsreader, log off and post replies at your leisure without running up internet access charges. When you were all done, you just logged back on for a second, uploaded your replies, and logged back off again—and so it went.

The first newsgroup I ever signed up for was *alt.christianity*. But it wasn't what I thought. It turned out to be a big debate arena for believers vs. atheists, and honestly, I became hooked on it. Of course, I debated against the atheists.

For me, like a passion, this went on for the next twenty years. When newsgroups faded out, MSN groups took over, and I was there. When they faded out, internet forums like *thinkingatheist.com* took over, and I went there to debate. Then Facebook came along and the discussions merged onto that platform with Facebook Groups.

During all that time, I became very knowledgeable about theistic philosophy, and I was good at arguing for the existence of God. I even invented a new argument for God's existence and won a Toastmasters International district speech contest using that very argument as the basis for a speech.

But, I remember the night I quit debating atheists. I just stopped, cold turkey, and never went back. I remember it clearly, because it changed my life, my way of thinking, and ultimately my spiritual destiny. I finally saw the truth: There is no God. There is no God, because God can't have a God.

Once I realized that, there was no point in debating. The atheists were right, but so was I, and all debates were necessarily fruitless from that point on.

Here's how I came to realize that God exists and doesn't exist at the same time. It goes like this:

If God was the first thing that ever existed, and logically he must be, then everything that exists after him had to come from his substance. In other words, he had to create it out of himself. As such, he must be the only material the universe is made from. This is pretty much the argument for *monism* put forward by the seventeenth century philosopher, Baruch Spinoza.

So, if everything is made from his substance, there can be no separation between things, for if there were, there would be a space between God and the separate thing. That space would neither be God nor be the thing he created. Even an infinitesimal line between God and the separate thing would still represent something that is neither God nor God's creation. And that separate thing would be a logical absurdity.

Note: A logical absurdity is a philosophical way of saying an impossibility, but it also has with it the idea of a contradiction. In other words, if something is absurd, it is not possible, because for it to be possible would imply a contradiction. For instance, a square circle, is an *absurd* notion, because it is inherently a contradiction. A square can't be a circle without ceasing to be a square.

Ironically, in Zen Buddhism, there is a form of meditation based on focusing on contradictions. The contradiction is called a *koan* (koh-an).

A koan is a short phrase that represents an absurdity. The idea of concentrating on the absurd contradiction is that it's supposed to lead to a transcendental state of mind where you understand things from a universal perspective, or what is often called, enlightenment.

A very common koan, which you've probably heard before, is "What is the sound of one hand clapping?" Even Jesus used a form of koan in his teachings when he said: *"If the light within you is darkness, how great is that darkness?"* (Matthew 6:23).

So, the idea of there being something in existence that is neither God nor a creation of God is an absurdity. In fact, spend enough time trying to imagine something that is neither God nor a creation of God, and you will find that you come to the transcendence of monism, and for me, the transcendence of monism is enlightenment.

So, if all things are connected by way of the substance of God, then God remains the only thing that ultimately exists. And, if God is the only thing that exists, then there is no God, because God can't have a God. In other words, God doesn't refer to anything as "God." The very word "God" implies something that is other than the one referring to it. In other words, God cannot point to something and say, "That is God."

Thus, since God is all there is, and there is nothing else. That means God exists, and there is no God. God exists without a God.

You must think on this for a bit for it to sink in. It's kind of like a koan. It seems like a contradiction, but when the contradiction resolves in your thinking, then you find enlightenment. It was certainly enough enlightenment for me that I stopped debating atheists. I stopped reading arguments for the existence of God. I stopped having "faith" in God—because I had found God.

And that enlightenment leads to the next axiom:

3. You are God and not God.

It goes without saying that if God is the only thing that really exists, then you must be God—because one thing you know for sure is that you exist.

Rene Descartes wrote in the seventeenth century: *Cogito ergo sum.* "I think; therefore, I am." He explained that phrase simply by arguing that we cannot doubt our existence while we are busy doubting it. To doubt our existence would be, as we mentioned before, an absurdity.

So, it hits us: If God was the first thing to exist, then God must be the only thing that exits, and if I exist without a doubt—then I am God.

The problem is that for being God, I feel quite powerless over most things in this world. In fact, most of us feel pretty powerless in our everyday lives. Why is that? If it's true that we are not just "a god" but "the God." Why do we have so little control over the events of our lives?

The answer is that you are God, and you are not God at the same time. I suppose that's another koan. And to understand this koan, we first must understand the nature of God, and then you'll see how it all relates back to you and this third axiom.

God's Nature

God's nature is everything. Our friend, Spinoza, argued that God has infinite attributes, and these attributes are expressed through an infinite number of modalities. I'll explain attributes and modalities below.

First, though, let me say that by infinite, we mean a modified concept of infinite. We mean all the attributes that can possibly exists and all the modalities that can possibly exist. A square circle can't really exist, so it's not an attribute or a modality of an attribute of God. Hot cold water can't exist, so it's not an attribute or a modality.

An attribute is a defining characteristic of God's Substance. Some examples of attributes might be, Space, Mind, Existence, etc. Not all the attributes are things we experience in the physical world. In fact, not all the attributes are even experienced on the astral plane. Because God is vastly larger than our physical universe, most of his attributes are completely hidden forever from humanity.

A modality is something that expresses an attribute in part. My finger is a modality of my body, and my body is an attribute of me. So, if Mind is an attribute of God, then consciousness is one of its modalities. If Space is an attribute of God, then shape is one of its modalities. An attribute can have many modalities. Space could also have movement, time, and distance as it's modalities. In the case of God's attributes, all the modalities that can belong to that attribute do belong to that attribute.

So, that brings us to you. You are a set of modalities. The one you're most concerned with, the one we are all most concerned with, is consciousness. You are conscious. That is a modality of the Divine attribute of Mind. Even more, you are astrologically unique. So, your modality of consciousness is an absolute. It's a one-of-a-kind, modality of the Divine attribute of Mind.

Therefore, you are God; however, your modality is not all God is. That makes you God and not God at the same time.

My finger is me. It's not just a part of me; it is fully fused into me. There is no line of separation that shows where it stops being me and starts being its own finger. It is me. Every cell has the same DNA as every other cell in my body. It is fully me, and yet, I am not just my finger. My finger is me and not me at the same time.

So, what I am describing to you about your nature, and I'll repeat it for good measure, is that you are God, but God is not just you, but you are all God. And this is the key to spiritual centering, which we will discuss in Chapter Four.

When you fully realize this—if you could fully realize this—it would mean that your consciousness would lose all other identity. Your modality would infuse back into the attribute of Mind, and then you would have all the powers of God.

You probably didn't learn this about God in Sunday school growing up. I know I didn't, but we're not talking about God in religious terms. We're talking about God in true terms. We're talking about the God of Everything, not just the god within the walls of a church or temple. And that brings us to our final axiom.

4. God is not religious.

The last thing we need to understand about God, or at least the last thing we need to understand to move forward with our psychic training, is that God and religion do not mix. Religion is about gods, not God.

We must be clear when we think about God, and the God we're talking about is not the God of any religious system. The God we're talking about that defines you and me and the rest of the universe by his very substance is utterly beyond human comprehension. So, there never has been a religion that ever had anything to do with him.

The best we can do with the capital G God is to stand in awe of him. As soon as we try to do anything else, like describe him, we instantly create a g-od out of G-od. As soon as we place a limit or shape on God, we instantly end up with a god that is not infinite, and is less powerful than he was before we limited him. We end up with our own idea of what God should be, not what God really is. Even calling God a "he" is an error, but what other pronoun would be any different? Unfortunately, the English language is inadequate for talking about God.

That said, creating our lowercase g god is necessary. We must, for our own sake, fashion God into something we can understand and deal with, or we have no target at all for our spiritual development.

If we don't create a god, we have nothing we can pray to. We have nothing we can commune with, and we have no way to understand our place in the world or our purpose in life. We, each one of us, must create a god of our own.

And, it's no sin to do it. It's a natural process of human psychology. Because we walk around every day experiencing our consciousness, but we get a sense that we are something more than that. We can't help but sense that there is a greater aspect to ourselves. We sense this greater aspect, because we are *of the substance* of God like we talked about in the previous section.

This sense of a higher self seems like something other than ourselves, because it is greater, and a lot wiser than our everyday mind here in the physical world. What we do with that sense of another/higher consciousness is a long word. We *anthropomorphize* our higher consciousness.

Anthropomorphosis means attributing human qualities to a non-human being or object. That's what we do with God. We can't handle God as God. In order to hold God in our mind, our mind would have to be as large as the entire Divine attribute of Mind, and if our mind was like that, we wouldn't even exist, because remember, we are a modality of that attribute. If you become the attribute, then you can no longer be a modality of it.

A good example of god-making is shown in the movie with Tom Hanks, *Cast Away*. In that movie, Hanks' character, Chuck Noland, is stranded on a remote island in the South Pacific after a plane crash. He is the only person on the island, and he's there for some four years all by himself.

At one point, he finds a volleyball that washed up from the planes debris field. He paints a face on it with his own blood and eventually starts talking to it. He names it, Wilson, because that's the brand of the ball, and he develops an entire relationship with it, so much so that when he loses it during his escape from the island, he grieves the loss of Wilson as much he would any human friend.

The point here is not to say that Chuck Noland went mad because he thought the ball was his friend; the point is that in his isolation, he separated part of his consciousness from himself and attributed it to the ball. The ball was alive to Noland, and since only Noland was on the island, he assumed the right to call the ball alive. And it was alive—Noland had given it life.

We do the same thing with our gods—and each one of us creates a personal god.

I understand this might sound atheistic, but it's not. God does exist. God is the only thing that exists. There is nothing but God. But God is a bit like Chuck Noland on the island. He has given us life from himself, and we backed it up a bit and split off our higher self into a god that we can pray to and worship. We give our god life, and in so doing, we can at least approach the big God a little more than we otherwise could.

Idolatry is Necessary

Now, the major world religions would call that idolatry. Surely, you know the first and second commandments: *I am the Lord thy God, thou shall have no other gods before me. Thou shalt not make unto thee any graven image, or any likeness of anything that is in heaven above, or that is in the earth beneath, or that is in the water under the earth.* (Exodus 20:1-4).

So, to make a god from your mind that stands in for the big God would be idolatry, but there's a problem with that. The problem is that the Ancient Israelites who wrote the ten commandments were making an idol out of God when they wrote the ten commandments. They could no more hold God in their minds back then than we can today. So, they made Jehovah or Yahweh as an idol of God, and then gave that idol to the people and commanded them not to make any other idol. It's really that simple.

So why should their idol be better than your idol? You're not even an Ancient Israelite. But the full weight of the authority of religion tends to crash in on our minds because of the force of civilization, and we tend to accept its authority and doubt our own ability to do what they did.

But it doesn't work, anyway. Because as I mentioned above, go to any church, sit down and have an honest talk with any member about God, and you will find a different definition of God given by each one.

So, God is not a religious concept. God is not a concept we can really understand at all. Therefore, unless we're going to live like godless, atheistic, hedonists on the planet earth—which is a psychologically unsustainable existence for most people—we will make our own god. My god is not your god. Your god is not for me. This is the way it's supposed to be, because there really is no single religion that can contain God. Perhaps the best religion, in that sense, would be one that recognized the big God, but then respected all the little gods and made room for them under one roof.

That brings us to the end of our axioms about God. It's important that you understand these things, or you won't have the foundation for the concepts we are about to discuss, but we still must talk about one other very important concept. That is the concept of our consciousness.

I'm conscious, and you're conscious, but there is a very damaging belief that is widely held about consciousness that we must clear up, or we will never develop as psychically self-realized people.

Chapter 3

Understanding Mind

In the previous chapter, we talked about God. Now we're going to back away from the overall concept of God and talk about one of his attributes, Mind.

The reason we must talk about Mind now is because human beings are modalities of Mind. Remember, what you really are is a mind, not a body. You are a psychic being and only incidentally physical.

Spirit and Mind are the same thing. The terms mean the same thing. You are a spirit in the physical world; that means you are a mind using a body in the physical world. But we have a serious problem: The common wisdom in the world today is the opposite. The common wisdom is that mind is a byproduct of the brain.

In other words, the accepted truth of things is that the physical gelatinous organ in your skull, by way of the bio-electrical and electrochemical properties of it, causes your mind to come to life. So, if you destroy the brain, the mind ceases to exist. That is the commonly accepted truth about the mind, but you will see below that nothing could be further from the truth.

An Emergent Mind?

This theory of a biocentric mind, which again is the accepted theory of the entire medical and scientific establishments, not to mention the general population at large, is called *emergence*. Emergence or emergentism, is the idea that your consciousness bubbles up from the workings of your brain. It then becomes an *epiphenomenon* of neuronal activity.

Those are some complex terms, but think of an epiphenomenon like a rainbow over a waterfall. The physical workings of the waterfall create a mist, and through the direction of sunlight through the mist, a rainbow "emerges." The rainbow over the waterfall is an epiphenomenon of the actions of the waterfall. The common notion of mind, therefore, is that it appears over your brain, so to speak, from the workings of your brain, just like a rainbow over a waterfall.

And what does that logically imply? It implies *nihilism*. Nihilism means that if you die, your consciousness dies as well—no life after death, no reincarnation, no visits to the astral plane, nothing, just the termination of existence.

Personally, it has taken me more than thirty years to get rid of the notion of emergentism, because it's a provable lie. Our minds do not require our brain.

Our minds need a brain to interact with a complex physical form like our bodies. It does need our brain to move that body around in the physical world and experience things of the world, but it doesn't need that brain to exist.

And it's not enough to just have faith in opposition to the idea of emergentism and nihilism. Religions have always taught that life goes on after death. They have always stressed the spiritual nature of man. But in this world, at this time, science is considered "the truth," not religious faith. And many people, even though they are religious, still believe the mind is generated by the brain, because science has taught them so for all of their lives.

It's not that I'm opposed to science. I'm opposed to partial, selective science standing in for the truth as it buries evidence to the contrary. So, I say let the whole scientific truth have the last word. I'm going to give you indisputable, repeatable, peer-reviewed, scientific proof that you can do yourself, if you want to, that shows the mind does not come from the brain.

Granted, afterward, we may not be able to understand what the mind exactly is. It may become a very mysterious thing, but it's supposed to be mysterious, and that's no different than many things we find in our universe.

We don't understand what gravity is—we know that it works, but we have no clue why or what it is. We don't know what electromagnetic force is—we know that it works, but we have no clue what it is. Through quantum physics, we observe how subatomic particles behave like magic, but we have no idea why they do. Those are indisputable facts of science—or should I say the lack of it. And now we are going to discuss some more indisputable observations that science has known about for a very long time, but you'll never see it mentioned in a textbook.

Our Friend, The Paramecium

In 2003, while I was in nursing school, I was required to take a class in microbiology. One night, the experiment was that we were to take a drop of pond water from a beaker that was full of pond water and algae. The instructor said she brought it from her own pond. Our assignment was to examine the protozoa we found using the microscope.

Protozoa are one-celled animals that live in the water. Technically, they are a diverse group of unicellular eukaryotic organisms. The favorite one to observe, because it's a little larger than most, and you can see all its internal structures, and because it's been studied for over 300 years, is the protozoan known as *Paramecium caudatum.*

I set up my slide that night with the pond water. My friend (and lab partner) wasn't having an easy time of it, but I was having some success that night. I prepared a good slide with a clear view of lots of paramecia all feeding on a tiny piece of algae. It was one of the better slides I'd ever prepared, and I sat there for a good half hour just watching the "Paramecium Show."

But then it hit me. All at once a sudden realization came out of the fog of my mind and stood in front of me like an unavoidable elephant in the room. The paramecium, specifically and most obviously the *Paramecium caudatum*, were making choices.

They were swimming around looking for food in one algae patch, then they would turn around and swim to another part of the patch and look for food there, then swim all the way across the drop and look for food there, then investigate this or that algae structure, only to then swim all the way back to where they had started—apparently remembering the spot they had come from. I even saw two paramecia swimming in a kind of coordinated dance. They did this kind of dance a lot, almost as if they were fighting, like the way dogs sometimes fight in a feeding frenzy.

On the surface, none of this was particularly amazing. My lab partner wasn't interested at all. And frankly, this behavior of paramecium has always been known. It's not like I'd discovered something new. But sitting there I asked myself a simple question: "Why did that paramecium just turn to the right?"

More to the point, *how* did it turn to the right? How does it make any decision at all? How is it obviously displaying will and desire? How is it able to remember where it was? Why is it displaying obvious mental functioning?

You see, we know everything about *Paramecium caudatum*. Literally, we know everything. We, the microbiology class, even studied it in one of the chapters of the textbook for that course. Science knows all the way down to the molecular structure how paramecium operates. We know every internal structure of that creature and how those internal structures work, and science has known most of this information for hundreds of years. There is no mystery to the *Paramecium caudatum* at all—except one: How does it make a choice?

Paramecium have no neurology whatsoever—nothing even remotely close to any kind of nervous system. No brain. No nerves. Their entire single-cell structure is nothing more than proteins, DNA, mitochondria, Golgi bodies, and maybe a few chemical enzymes. There is nothing in their structure that can account for their undeniably conscious will. So, how did it turn to the right that night under my microscope?

That night it hit me like a ton of bricks, and it changed my life forever. Paramecia have a mind, but they have no nervous system. They have a simple mind for sure, but they have one, and they have no brain. Hence, the mind cannot come from the brain. And that night, before me, was the scientific fact of it.

When I made the connection, I brought it up to my friend. He thought it was interesting—for about ten seconds. So, I tried showing other classmates and asking them those same questions about the little critters (How did the paramecium turn right?), but mostly all I got was shoulder shrugging. No one knew the answer, but moreover, no one really seemed to care either, and I couldn't believe how it couldn't be hitting them like it was hitting me.

Time went on, but I didn't forget what I'd witnessed in that class. A year later, I bought my own medical microscope so I could continue to do the experiment at home. But now, anyone can go and view them without a microscope just by searching YouTube for "paramecia feeding on algae." There were only a couple videos at first, but now there are lots of them. It's much easier and cheaper to use YouTube than it is to set up a microscope and prepare a slide—even if not as fun in my opinion.

But when you view them, just focus on one and watch its behavior. You'll see that it is making choices in its movement. But to make a choice requires a will, and will (also called *volition*) is a function of mind.

For years, I thought I was alone in my observations. I tried to talk about it in online forums, but those forums were mostly atheist debate forums, so the atheists therein were not about to accept that a mind could exist outside of a brain, and especially rest that proof in lifeforms as insignificant to them as paramecia.

The resistance I encountered centered mostly on my not being a scientist, and therefore, probably, simply, not knowing what I was talking about. But then I made my next discovery which was nearly as shocking to me as when I first saw the paramecia. Again, this was nothing that I ever found in any microbiology textbook.

Training the Brainless

It turns out scientists had been training paramecia for about a hundred years. Thanks to the phenomenal blossoming of information on the internet, in 2008, I came across a scientific paper written by Harvard L. Armus, Amber R. Montgomery, and Jenny L. Jellison from the University of Toledo.

The paper is titled, *Discrimination Learning in Paramecia (P. caudatum)*, and was published in *The Psychological Record* (2006, Issue 56, pages 489-498). The paper detailed experiments they had done that confirm the validity of experiments that had been conducted, going all the way back to 1911, where paramecia were found to be capable of learning through classical conditioning.

Classical conditioning is also known as stimulus-response training. For instance, an animal can be trained to respond in a certain way each time a stimulus is given followed by a reward.

You can train a dog to sit anytime it hears the refrigerator open. But such conditioning requires a mind. If a dog sits when it hears the refrigerator open, it must be deciding to sit as opposed to standing. It's not like some physical process took place making the dog sit against its will. It doesn't unconsciously sit like a robot. It acquired knowledge through the stimulus of the refrigerator door being tied to a food treat, and it chooses to sit so it can get the treat. But that is all conscious activity.

You can't train something that's unconscious. You can only train something that possesses consciousness, and consciousness requires a mind. Dogs have a mind, and dogs have a brain, so one could assume the mind comes from the brain. Unless there is a creature that has no brain and yet displays obvious mental activity, then you must conclude the mind is independent of the brain.

The research by Armus, et. al., showed that paramecia can be trained. Briefly, the paramecia were trained to move down a tube toward a light anytime an electrical stimulus was applied, because each time they did, they found food (bacteria). Eventually, they would move down the tube any time the light was applied.

I can't publish the actual research paper in this book, because it belongs to the *Psychological Record*. But since 2008, I've noticed more and more references to the research paper on the web. If you just search "Discrimination Learning in Paramecium," you'll surely find it. It's free, and I have the .pdf downloaded on my computer. You can download it, too.

Now, perhaps this isn't such a big deal on the surface, but the implications of it are staggering: not only do paramecia have volition; they apparently have memory as well. You can't train something that has no memory. Memory and will are the hallmarks of consciousness, but *P. caudatum* have no nervous system whatsoever. Where then is the consciousness coming from?

The research doesn't venture a guess at the metaphysical implications. It doesn't make speculations about where the consciousness is coming from; it only shows that paramecium can be trained. The implication, however, the 800-pound gorilla in the room, is the realization that paramecium have no physical mechanism that can generate the mind that is required to do the training.

So, what does this have to do with you, and what does it have to do with defining what you are?

Consider this: People look in the mirror, and they think that's who and what they are. They think they are their body, and their mind is up in their heads generated by their brains. And if the brain dies, the person dies. That's the common understanding of our nature. So, we fear death, and we live according to the flesh, and we live like physical-first people.

But if paramecia, without any nervous system whatsoever, are obviously conscious, it is reasonable to assume your consciousness is not a product of your brain. Why would it be? Apparently, consciousness exists in trillions of little creatures found in ponds all over the earth who have no brain at all.

The Brain as a Receiver

There has always been a debate about the human mind. No one really knows where it comes from. Consciousness is the most common phenomenon known to humankind, because everyone experiences it, but no one really knows what it is.

Since the nineteenth century, since the dawning of modern science, it has always been assumed that it comes from the workings of the brain. After all, if you kill the brain of a person, they don't move anymore, and they die. But it's just not that simple.

First, there has never been a scientific explanation for how the firings of neurons in the brain can produce the phenomenon of we know as consciousness. It's just *assumed* that it works that way.

Second, there is no way to know whether our consciousness is coming from our brain or just being received by the brain, the same way a television doesn't produce a TV program but acts as a receiver of the TV signal that is broadcasting the program.

There have always been these two possibilities existing side by side: either the brain produces consciousness or it receives consciousness. But with paramecium, the question is answered: there is consciousness even when there is no brain. So, consciousness is not produced by the brain. Creatures with bigger bodies, apparently, just need a brain so they can do more things with their bigger bodies in the physical world.

And what does that tell us? For one, it tells us there is absolutely no reason to think consciousness stops when the body and brain dies. In other words, the paramecium studies give clear and convincing evidence that consciousness is an external thing. Our bodies are not generating it. Our bodies are being used by it, just as the paramecium bodies are used by it.

So, it's no longer a matter of mere faith to say you believe you will live after you die. The scientific fact is that there is no good reason to think the real you—the mind of you—has anything to do with your physical body. It appears you are using your body just like you use a screwdriver or hammer. Your body is a tool of your mind. Kill the body, and the mind simply loses its ability to perceive and manipulate the physical world.

All of this is written in aid of one thing: to convince you that you are a psychic being first and foremost and not just a physical body. The permanent you is not the body you see in the mirror. It is the mind that uses that body. When you fully realize this, the whole world of spiritual reality will open up for you.

Unit Two

Essential Psychic Skills

———————— • —————————

The purpose of this section is to provide you with a basic set of tools you'll need to start your journey toward psychic self-realization. No matter what psychic art you choose to practice (and we will discuss those arts in the next section), understanding the basics of these spiritual practices is key to developing your psychic self.

Now that you've grasped the concepts of what you are, who God is, and where the mind comes from, you are ready to learn the three fundamental skills of spirituality: centering, grounding, and shielding. So, let's begin!

Chapter 4

Centering

———— • ————

Centering means achieving a state of mind that brings into focus your essential nature. It is self-realization, and it is achieved through understanding three fundamental facts about your existence, and then reinforcing those facts in your mind with a meditational exercise. The three fundamental facts are:

1. You are alone. (Isolation)

2. You are the center of the universe. (Unification)

3. Your purpose is to ascend. (Ascension)

Think of centering as a pyramid. To center, you must move through each level of the pyramid until you reach the very top. The idea is that you cannot skip a step, because one leads naturally to the other. For instance, you cannot realize the truth of unification until you first realize the truth of isolation, and you can't realize your purpose is to ascend to the Divine unless you have first realized isolation and unification.

The purpose of the meditational exercise is to progress through the facts in your mind until you reach ascension, and thus become centered. It is the knowledge of the facts that brings the centering, and it is the meditation, which we will look at below, that reinforces the knowledge.

If the meditation is practiced regularly, then over time, the facts will become part of your reality, and then centering can be turned on like a switch whenever you need it.

So, with that said, let's examine each of the facts, and then learn the meditation technique of centering.

Fact 1: You are alone.

This is the foundation of the pyramid. It's not a pleasant realization; it's not supposed to be. But until it is realized, ascension is not possible. Once it is realized, only then can the sadness it brings be dealt with and cleared.

We spend a great deal of our lives with other people. As kids, we are with our siblings and parents. As adults, we are with our spouses and partners. In old age, if we're lucky, we have our children and grandchildren around us. But even so, we are alone.

No matter how well we know someone; no matter how close our proximity to them, even during sexual intercourse, we are alone. We are alone, because everything we experience is experienced in our own individual way.

Two people looking at a sunset see it differently. Even if they are sitting next to each other, even if they are holding each other, even though they are seeing it at the same time, they are experiencing it alone. This realization of utter aloneness is the broad foundation of the pyramid.

Typically, the notion that we are fundamentally alone is universally rejected and avoided at all costs. Loneliness is considered bad. We consider it tragic if someone dies alone. A lone existence is considered pathetic and even torturous.

In prison, the harshest punishment is solitary confinement. In solitary confinement, the prisoner is not physically mistreated, but he or she is left alone for long periods of time. This, presumably, causes great distress. And yet, in one sense, we are all in solitary confinement: the physical world is the solitary confinement of our souls, because we experience life alone.

Of course, there is the argument that love conquers that. That love is what turns two into one. It's considered the antidote to loneliness. But love doesn't really make us one. Therein lies the melancholy of this foundational, pyramid-bottom truth. Love does not vanquish isolation.

In fact, love requires isolation. Love is what we want from other people. We, as solitary individuals, want to be important to someone else. We want to believe someone cares about our wellbeing. We want someone with us to help us and to share in our moments of grief and in our moments of happiness and joy. We want someone other than ourselves to be with us to watch a sunset. But if we were actually one with that other person, then once again we'd be alone.

The existence of love, and moreover, *the desire for love*, proves that we are fundamentally isolated from one another. There would be no need for love if we were not alone. But we are alone, and the whole concept of love requires that we are.

The realization of isolation brings with it a necessary sadness. It's supposed to. It's supposed to bring you down, make you feel sad, fill you with despair and existential angst. It's supposed to make you depressed. Because the way up the pyramid is through the foundation, not around it. So much of life is used up trying to make up for the feeling of loneliness. All human relationships center on eliminating loneliness, but the way up is through loneliness, not through avoiding it.

But even more than just suffering the sadness of isolation, we must embrace it. We can't squint our eyes and steel ourselves mentally, and then take as small of dose as possible. Rather, we must welcome it with open arms and open eyes. We must not let ourselves become inebriated with ideas, whatever they may be, that help us avoid or ignore it. Because only by stepping on the foundation of the pyramid, and applying our whole emotional weight to it, can we climb it and reach the next fundamental fact.

Fact 2: You are the center of the universe.

When I say that you are the center of the universe, I mean it quite literally: you are the actual center of the entire universe. The realization of this truth is the next level of the pyramid.

It follows necessarily from the foundation of being utterly alone. No one shares this universe with you, so everyone you see or meet is appearing, for some reason, in your universe. Consider for a moment that you cannot even verify that any other person or animal is conscious. They could simply be objects, no different than rocks, or trees, or stars. You are only aware of your own consciousness. Granted, the people you see and the animals you encounter appear conscious, but you have no way to prove that they really are, or if they are like dream-people and only giving the appearance of consciousness. You literally have no solid reason to believe there is anything alive in the universe except for you.

Added to this, the universe is infinite in all directions. If you were to get in a spaceship and race to the edge of the universe, the journey would never end, and it doesn't matter which way you go. So, for all intents and purposes, you are, geographically, the center of the universe. And everything that occurs in the universe is happening around you. Moreover, near as you can tell, it is happening for you.

What we are talking about is a fundamental characteristic of existence. In the previous chapter, we talked about the monistic nature of God. That is, that God is the only thing that exists, and you are only God. God is not only you, but you are only God. And as such, you are the monistic substance of the only thing that exists. You are alone, and as such you are the eternal center of everything. The universe literally occurs and revolves around you.

You could even argue that it is you who wrote this book. You wrote it for you, to wake yourself up. I am merely a technique your mind is using—the image of an author writing a book that you will read, but in fact, it is only you, as the monistic substance of God, who wrote the book for yourself.

Now, of course, *I* don't believe that. I believe that the universe centers on me, and so does every other living creature that has a mind, even the paramecia we talked about in the last chapter. We all believe the exact same thing. Moreover, it doesn't matter what anyone else believes. We are all the centers of the universe—our own universe.

Why should anyone believe that an infinite Divine Creator created only one universe? If he can create one, he can create an infinity of universes—one for each modality of his Mind. That means one for each conscious creature he makes. When you come to see it this way, then you will come to see that you and the universe are just one thing. You and the universe are one single, solitary life form. And that is *unification.*

This second level requires acceptance. The emotional experience of this fundamental truth becomes a feeling of acceptance. It replaces the sadness of the first truth. It's not really a good feeling, though it may be a relief from the despair of being alone, but it's not happiness either; it's just neutral.

When you come to realize that you are the center of the universe, when you come to feel that everything that happens is happening around you, and for you, it doesn't make you feel as if you have gained anything. Any sense of grandeur or narcissistic entitlement that would come from being the one and only being the universe exists for is tempered by the fact that you are alone in it.

At the same time, realizing you are the center of the universe brings about an expansion of mind. As you contemplate it, it becomes quite difficult to stay grounded. As you contemplate it in meditation, you may find that your mind begins to travel. It may travel first to places you know on earth, but then you may begin to reach out to the moon, perhaps Mars or Venus. And then you may find that you are traveling across the vastness of space to places no one knows. This is the experience of astral travel. And it is generally considered a pleasurable experience.

Nevertheless, we soon find that the melancholy of being alone is tempered by the realization of being the center of the universe, and the resulting emotion is one of acceptance. This acceptance is necessary for the realization of the final, top level of the pyramid of facts.

Fact 3: Your purpose is ascension.

People spend a lot of their lives trying to figure out what their purpose is in life. Of course, this is primarily physical-first thinking, because we wonder most about what we are supposed to do here on the earth. Should we have this or that career? Should we give our lives to this or that cause? We try to choose the right path, because we realize that we have a limited time on earth, and we want to make the most of it. We want to be all that we can be and perhaps leave some kind of legacy behind us.

In astrology, this is called a *tenth house issue*, and a person can look to the tenth house in their horoscope to analyze why they were born. The tenth house is all about what kind of mark we are going to make on the world.

But, when it comes to centering, we aren't talking about our purpose in the world. Once the first two foundational truths are realized, our purpose during the relatively brief time we have on earth becomes proportionally meaningless.

Once you realize that you are alone, and then realize that being alone places you at the center of the universe, it's natural to then wonder what purpose you really have. What reason is there for your consciousness to even exist? Being a lawyer and, let's say, defending people who are hurt by injustice may be an important tenth house issue for you, but it pales in comparison to why your consciousness remains for eternity alone at the center of the universe. The answer to that existential question requires *ascension.*

Ascension is the process whereby a modality of consciousness (You could call that modality, "personhood.") comes into a fuller awareness of being God, and thus transforms from a modality into the Divine attribute of Mind. During ascension, all ego is stripped away, and the person exists less and less the more they transform into Mind.

Ascension is the purpose of our modality. What that means is that you, as a modality, have always had only one purpose. As soon as you were created as a person, from the modality of consciousness, from the Divine attribute of Mind, the whole idea was that you would gradually come to realize once again that you are that Mind. You would ascend from personhood to God. And, apparently, this is something God finds quite pleasurable.

When you think about it, it only makes sense: If God is everything, if all things come from the substance of God, if God is the only thing that truly exists, then God represents the ultimate perfection in all things.

As you ascend in your awareness that you really aren't just Jane or John Doe, but are in fact, God, and as the identity of Jane or John Doe strips away, you are transformed into the perfection of God. And this is the fundamental definition of pleasure. The bottom line is that you were created with the sole purpose of ascending back into the attribute of God from whence you came, because the process creates a pleasure that God experiences through you.

There are no good or complete examples of this on the earth. You won't find any. But there are hints of it, and there are symbols of it: A child seeks to transform into an adult. A fool seeks to transform into a wise person. The process of evolution, apparently, seeks the perfect fit of a species into its environment. A caterpillar changes into a butterfly. A great work of art is created from the progressive refinement of cruder forms. (A lump of clay becomes a statue; chords become a song; raw paint becomes a portrait.) When you come to realize this process of transformation applies to your consciousness as well, the process of ascension begins.

Through ascension, who you are when you look in the mirror becomes less relevant. Eventually, everything you've ever done in your life becomes a series of minor events. Then you start to realize that all the lives through which you have incarnated have only served to bring you to this place of ascension. Then you start to understand that all the pleasure you've ever sought out or experienced has been a mere stand-in for the ascension that you had not yet found. And the more you ascend, the more you enter that eternal bliss.

The corresponding emotional state of this is joy. When you started centering and realized you were utterly alone, you found only despair and melancholy. Then, when you accepted it, you found yourself at the center of the universe. Now, that acceptance has turned into the joy of greater things to come.

You exist to ascend into the perfection of Mind, and this means that all the suffering you've endured has happened for a good reason. One way or another, it has brought you to the point of ascension. No matter how bad things get, you know that ascension waits for you, and you can begin to participate in it any time you want to. This is the top of the pyramid of centering.

And ascension never ends. You were created as a modality so that you eternally ascend. The more you ascend the greater the pleasure. The closer you get to the Divine attribute of Mind, the more bliss you experience, and thus, the more bliss God experiences through you.

If you are mathematically inclined, this is seen in the concept of a limit that approaches infinity. It's a calculus concept, and it's very simple: Just imagine a process that describes a distance that gets smaller and smaller but never gets to zero. The closer you get, the stronger it gets, but it never gets to the end. It just gets infinitely stronger. And that's how it is: the closer you get to Mind, the greater the bliss, but for all eternity, you are always approaching it, you are never actually getting there. This is the concept of infinite bliss. This is what comes from ascension, and it represents the joy of purpose. Ascension is why God created you.

A Meditation for Centering

So, those are the fundamental facts of centering. And there is a three-step meditation exercise you can do to help you center—that is to help you realize the truth of the fundamental facts of centering. And you should practice this meditation at least once a day, or if you prefer, you can do it at night before you fall asleep, or you can do it before you begin practicing a psychic art. It's highly effective for orienting a person toward a psychic identity.

Step 1: Isolate

In this step, it's important to get alone somewhere and try to remove distractions from your environment. This could be when you take a walk, when you lie down to sleep, when you're in the bathtub or shower or wherever. If you really want to experience it profoundly, put on a backpack and go camping in some remote wilderness for a day or two. The point is, whatever you need to get yourself physically away from the distractions of other people is what you should do.

Then just think about it. That's all there is to this step—thinking: Allow the reasons you are alone to come into your mind. Some of them will seem like self-pity, but that's perfectly fine. It doesn't matter. You must come to the awareness that you are alone in the universe.

Some of those reasons might be that no one else can know your thoughts. No one cares how you feel. Everyone will choose themselves over you. You can't prove anyone else is conscious. You will die alone. Your kids don't call. Your mother favors your sister. Whatever evidence you have, tell it to yourself until you start to feel the isolation from it.

When you first practice this step, and for however long it takes for you to come to psychological terms with it, you will feel down about it. It will make you sad; it may even lead to a period of depression in your life. That's to be expected. This first step is not easy. For it to work, you must believe it, and you may not believe it now, and it could take time before you do. We live with many layers of delusion in our minds to protect us from the melancholy of this truth. So, it may take time.

But eventually, as you perform this first step, you will no longer feel anything. There will simply be the knowledge in your mind that you exist alone in the world. You won't like it, but you will understand it. Accomplishing the isolation step, at that point, will be a simple matter of reminding yourself of it, and you can then move straight into Step 2.

Step 2: Unify

The Gospel of Thomas is a gnostic gospel that was discovered in a cave at Nag Hammadi in Egypt in 1945. It was written around 140 AD, and it is supposed to contain

114 sayings of Jesus. Most people attracted to New Age spirituality love it, but of course, it's not part of the bible. Nevertheless, in the seventy-seventh verse of the *Gospel of Thomas*, Jesus said the following:

I am the Light that is over all things. I am the All. From me All has come forth; and to me, All is returned.

To accomplish *unification*, memorize and meditate on these words as if you are the one who originally said them. Study the passage above until each word matters to you and opens its significance to you.

Jesus, in the *Gospel of Thomas*, is a symbol of what humankind is meant to be. So, if you want them to be, these really are your words. It's a short passage to memorize. Put it on your refrigerator door; put it on your bathroom mirror. The more you read it and say it, the more the truth of it will become part of you.

To complete this step, get comfortable. You don't have to get into any kind of special sitting posture or yoga position. You can, if that's what you like to do, but you don't have to. You can light candles, sit in a darkened room, light incense, whatever you want to do, but the goal is just to relax the mind for a moment. You should eventually be able to do so even in a crowded room or elevator.

Close your eyes, and inhale deeply through your nose, all the way as far as you can. Hold it for a few seconds, then begin to exhale. Exhale as slowly as you can without causing respiratory panic. If you feel like you want to take a breath, exhale faster until that feeling goes away.

As you are exhaling, say the mantra in your mind, and see yourself sitting in space in the center of the universe.

Visualize a soft blue light emanating from you and forming all the planets and stars around you.

Stay in this state for as long as you feel like staying in it, but when you're ready, open your eyes and glance upon some minor inanimate object: an object on the floor, a piece of litter perhaps, or even your own shoe, it could be anything at all. The important thing is to feel the connection. You are the *All*, and from you *All* has come forth. When you feel the connection with the inanimate object that you are looking at, imagine that it has come from you and is an extension of your substance.

Stay in this state for as long as you need to. Some people remain here without taking the next step, because it is a very peaceful and comfortable place to be, and it makes being isolated okay. It is a state of acceptance, and it is very restful.

In truth, a lot of psychic practice can be done from this state of mind, especially the art of astral projection or remote viewing, clairvoyance, mediumship, even spellcasting, and faith-healing, or if one were to challenge themselves with Zener ESP cards, or conduct laboratory experiments related to psi ability, this state of mind would yield the greatest results. It's psychically very powerful; however, it's not the goal of centering. There is still one more step in this meditation.

Step 3: Ascend

After you isolate and unify, the next step is to ascend. This is accomplished while you are still in a state of unification. Simply tilt your head back, with your eyes still open, and visualize yourself, leaving your body through your eyes and shooting upward. Don't tilt your head so much that it hurts your neck and distracts you, just try to look up comfortably. You could always do this entire meditation lying down, and then you wouldn't have to look up or down at all.

That said, ascending is best accomplished if you can look up at the sky, either during the day or at night, but it can be done anywhere and still work to some degree. The sensation is one of astral projection.

As you experience ascension, you will notice you will begin to lose the connection to yourself. You will begin to feel neutral in personality. This is the falling away of your ego identity. It's not that you stop existing, or that your consciousness fades, quite the opposite. It is an expansion of your consciousness. Technically speaking, it is the modality transforming into the attribute. And during this expansion, it simply won't matter to you anymore who you are. That is the ego falling away.

Because ascension is a state of mind where your consciousness expands into attribute of Divine Mind, some people find it very pleasurable to practice. In fact, it can become somewhat addictive. A great deal of psychic phenomena can occur from this state of mind, but you may not actually want to do any psychic practice. You may simply want to remain in ascension and do nothing. And this phenomenon leads to the concluding section of this chapter, which is a warning about centering.

The Danger of Over-Centering

Put simply, centering is not compatible with the psychology needed to function in the physical world. It can be used as a tool to decrease stress, realize the truth, and enhance psychic abilities, but just like any medication can help us in prescribed doses, if it is over-used, it can hurt us. The same is true with centering.

If a person centers too much, they will begin to form a habit of losing connection with their physical life. The things of physical life just won't matter as much. To the outside observer, this could appear as a kind of psychosis.

Psychosis and Centering

Psychosis is a state of mind where one cannot tell what is real from what is not real. They often hallucinate and hear things that aren't there. They may also see things that are not there. They may become obsessed with irrational ideas, and they may stop caring for themselves. They may neglect their hygiene, choose to live on the streets, isolate from other human beings, and flatten emotionally.

A person who centers often, and especially after they get good at it, will connect easily with the astral plane. So, they may hear things from there, see things from there, and ignore what's going on in the physical world. The feeling of ascension can be addictive. Therefore, as you can see, this would be indistinguishable from a psychotic break. Even though it's not psychosis, even though it is the highest functioning of mind, a person's family members, perhaps their doctor, or a psychiatrist, would have no way to differentiate it from mental illness.

Therefore, centering is a tool to be used only by those wise enough to use it with restraint. It should not be taught to those who already have serious mental health issues. The wise practitioner knows that centering can be used to enhance psychic abilities, but over-centering is to be avoided. And that wisdom is founded on the understanding that we need to remain in the world for the lifespan we are given to spiritually mature for a better life on the astral plane when we cross over.

Fortunately, however, there is an antidote to over-centering. And that is the subject of the next chapter.

Chapter 5

Grounding

Maybe you've heard the expression: "Don't be so heavenly-bound that you're no earthly good." I used to hear it in church from time to time as I was growing up. In other words, don't get so spiritual that you can't connect with everyday people in your life. In metaphysical terms, we call it *grounding*.

The human mind is capable of great spiritual connections to the astral plane and to the Divine. The problem is that such connections are not compatible with living in the physical world. Taken to an extreme, a person can become so spiritual-minded that they lose all desire to be alive in the physical world. This could be quite dangerous if depression were to set in as a result.

Centering, as we discussed in the last chapter, is intended to put a person's mind in communion with the Divine Mind through ascension. Centering is used to empower psychic abilities, to realize the truth of our existence, and to alleviate the anxiety of death, but it must be balanced with grounding, or it can sweep us away. Think of it like a helium balloon. If you don't keep it secured to the ground, it will take off and end up lost forever.

Grounding reverses the experience of centering. The purpose of grounding is to keep you connected to the physical world so you can operate in it and learn the lessons you were incarnated to learn. We are not in the physical world for the span of our lives simply to avoid it or escape it. We are here for a reason.

The relationship of centering to grounding is seen in the yin-yang symbol. The more one centers, the greater the need for grounding, and the more one grounds, the greater the need for centering.

There really is no gray area or middle ground one can achieve as a solution to the dichotomy of centering and grounding. Rather one flows into the other in a continuous cycle. We center to avoid over-grounding, we then ground to avoid over-centering.

When to Ground

You should ground after each centering meditation, because centering can leave you feeling *dissociated*. Dissociation is a sensation that you are not in your body, or that somehow your body and the world around you are not real. It's a feeling of detachment. Often there is a kind of fogginess of the mind that accompanies it.

Centering dissociation may also occur after practicing the psychic arts. Mediumship (connecting with spirits that have crossed over), is a frequent cause of centering dissociation. But the various forms of divination can lead to it as well: reading tarot cards, concentrating on pendulum readings, scrying (gazing into a crystal ball), or automatic writing. In fact, most of the psychic arts will lead to centering dissociation after practicing them for a stretch. So, look for the basic symptoms of centering dissociation, and use that as a sign that it's time to ground:

- Mental fogginess
- Feeling sleepy
- Forgetfulness or amnesia
- Feeling low or depressed
- Feeling that the world is unreal
- Not recognizing yourself in a mirror
- Uncontrollable daydreaming
- Staring blankly (a.k.a., sluggish cognitive tempo)

Four Methods of Grounding

Fortunately, for our survival in the world, the Divine Mind has made some methods of grounding a natural occurrence in our daily lives. Clearly this was designed into our nature to keep us functioning in the world. Other methods of grounding are voluntary. You may have your own favorite method already, but here are some methods that are proven to work for anyone:

1. Sleep

Sleep is the number one method of grounding. Ironically, the mind is less bound by its incarnation during sleep and can partially travel in the astral realm in the form of dreaming, but the body, especially the neurology of the central nervous system resets during sleep. So, when a person wakes up, they wake up and mentally take in the physical world as if it were a first sensation—this results in grounding.

So, if you've just finished a long bout of psychic practice, or if you've had a strong ascension during centering meditation, if you're feeling the symptoms of centering dissociation, just go to sleep. Lay down and take a nap. When you wake up, you will almost certainly be grounded.

2. Physical Pleasure

A hot bath, a massage, aroma therapy, good music, food, sex, sunbathing, swimming, really the list could go on, and you can use your own desires and imagination to fill in the blanks. The point is that physical pleasure has a way of jerking a person out of centering and into the physical world. Through physical pleasure, the mind becomes focused on the physical world, and grounding occurs.

So, if you're feeling foggy, light some incense, put on a good record, and have some chocolate. This will certainly bring you down to earth, so to speak. But I want to focus on two of these physical pleasures, food and sex, because they can be a burden and a blessing at the same time when it comes to grounding.

Food

Healthy food nourishes the body. We must eat if we are going to live in the physical world. But as we all know, there is an epidemic of obesity in the Western World. This is the result of the absolute need for food that God designed into us meeting the absolute availability of vast quantities of inexpensive, high-calorie food.

Eating produces grounding. So, it can be used to counter the effects of centering, but over-eating leads to a state where one never centers at all. And this leads to spiritual diminishment.

God made it so we had to eat, so we couldn't just float away in ascension and thus never accomplish the learning of this life. Our responsibility is to manage that form of grounding, use it for pleasure and nourishment, but show restraint so that it doesn't overtake our lives and create a situation of permanent grounding. As the old saying goes: We want to eat to live, not live to eat.

Sex

Sex is a powerful grounding force. There is a reason why mystics and priests are often celibate, and it's to prevent the iron grip of grounding that sex generates. I am not advocating celibacy, but we must look at how our sexual nature can prevent spiritual advancement. Because if we at least look at it, then we won't be fooled by it. Then we can indulge in it all we want, because we are fully aware of the dosage we are taking. If we are aware, then we can make an informed choice, and that's all this sub-chapter is about—allowing you to make an informed choice.

Consider this: When a child comes into the world, they tend to have more psychic experiences. They see more ghosts than adults do; they remember past lives more of-ten; they have visitations from the astral realm. (Sometimes we call them imaginary friends.) They have more vivid dreams, and they have a greater sense of faith—but then comes puberty.

Once an adolescent becomes sexually mature, their entire world tends to revolve around sexual desire in one way or another. It controls how they dress, how they act, the persona they adopt, the short-range goals they set, and the people they hang out with. They confuse sexual desire with love, and it energizes them with purpose and mean-ing, and they begin to date and usually have sexual rela-tions at some point before they reach any level of psycho-logical maturity that would give them an objective view of what it all means.

Even if they aren't dating and their sexual activity cen-ters on fantasy and self-gratification, their mind is still completely pre-occupied with it. As a result, their spiritu-ality is neglected, and they become physical-first people overnight, or so it seems.

Nevertheless, this is all as it should be. The Divine made it that way in a sense to trap humanity into a physi-cal existence, because the Divine wants people to live out a physical life on earth. If the pleasure of sex, and the deception of sexual desire as love, didn't trap us, we'd probably stop having sex altogether in favor of centering. And as a result, humans would die out very quickly. Apparently, the Divine Mind just doesn't want that to happen.

And realize, it's not just the act of sexual intercourse or the resulting orgasm that are at issue here. It's the entire concept of love. Most people who are physical-first consider love and sexual desire to be one in the same. Lust equates to falling in love, and even though most people intellectually know the difference, they still don't understand it emotionally. The desire to have sex with someone often gets treated the same as being in love with that person.

What follows is what is considered to be perfectly natural: marriage, children, a job that supports the household, and if the marriage is lagging, perhaps another child to help cement things back together—which means more secular work, more time spent caring for the children, etc. And this grounding becomes utterly complete.

There is no time for disconnecting or centering. There is no way to see that one is truly alone (which if you remember is the first step in centering). Meditation, if it is practiced at all, becomes a mere physical technique used to release the tension of everyday life. This lifestyle is so grounding, and it is such a pervasive social phenomenon throughout the world, that it is rare to meet anyone who is truly spiritual. Self-realized psychic people are the sanctified exception to the rule of life.

I have no prescription for this. Sex is not a problem to be solved. The resultant grounding is intended by the Divine. It is clearly not a good thing if all of humankind decided to be celibate and no one had children anymore. Thus, the problem is not solved by adopting its opposite.

Rather, you simply must be aware of the grounding effect of sex and all that sex implies. Just being aware, just understanding it, is itself a meditation that can lead to greater enlightenment.

And of course, there is the positive side. Sexual activity is in fact an absolute antidote to the effects of centering. It can absolutely be used for that purpose. It is a sure form of grounding.

3. *Competitive Exercise*

Another form of grounding that is both healthy and fun is competitive exercise. By competitive, I mean that you must be competing with yourself or someone else. If you are riding a bike or running, you should be looking to gradually go father or faster. If you are swimming, you should be gradually trying to go longer. Any physical exercise that you are doing, you should be looking to beat what you did previously if you are looking to use it for grounding.

The reason the exercise must be competitive is that otherwise it can easily turn into an environment conducive to centering. For instance, if one is used to walking a mile every day, and they walk that mile every day, eventually, they will be well-conditioned for that exercise, and it can easily allow the mind to wander. If the mind wanders, it can become dissociated and the effects of centering can take hold. If the exercise is competitive, with yourself of with others, you will stay focused on your time, your distance, how tired you are, and the achievement of some physical goal. That creates the effects of grounding.

And this competitiveness can be very gradual and still work, because it's not the results that matter, it's the competition. Nor does it matter what level of fitness you are at. Physical rehabilitation after some accident or disease can have enormous grounding effects. If all you can do is walk a mile, then try running a few steps before starting to walk, then every so often increase that by a couple of steps. It can be that gradual. All that matters is that the exercise remain physical work, and that it doesn't become so routine that you end up centering while doing it.

4. Meditative Grounding

A common notion of grounding is that it's a type of spiritual meditation. The idea is that grounding connects you to the energy of the earth, thus keeping you from depleting your own vital energy.

Essentially, you connect with the earth by visualizing yourself connecting to the earth through roots that extend down from your feet into the earth like a tree. And like a spiritual tree, you visualize the energy of the earth moving up through those roots and into your being.

This visualization is often accomplished during yoga practice, or you may simply close your eyes, take a deep breath and exhale slowly; quiet your mind, and visualize the roots extending from your tailbone (the location of your root chakra), down through your legs, out through your feet and into the ground. Then as you inhale, visualize the earth energy flowing up into you, and as you exhale, visualize your roots going deeper into the earth.

That is the basics of meditative grounding. I mention it because it is a very popular method of grounding, but I mention it last because I'm not a big proponent of it. The reason I'm not a proponent of meditative grounding is because rather than countering the effects of centering, it tends to increase them. Certainly, the goal of practical and meditative grounding is the same. Both seek to draw energy from the earth, but the method is what differs.

Practical grounding literally joins one to the physical plane by deliberately distracting the mind from its spiritual nature. Meditative grounding reinforces one's spiritual nature, as a minimum, by focusing on the root chakra. Also, the visualization of roots extending into the earth is identical to the unification step in the centering meditation where one visualizes all the planets and stars as emanating from their substance.

So, while I recognize meditative grounding as pervasive in the metaphysical community, I cannot endorse its efficacy for spiritual balance. Ultimately, however, you will have to decide for yourself which way is best for you. I suggest trying both ways and seeing what results you come up with.

Over-Grounding

Just as in centering, there is a danger in over-grounding. The effects of over-grounding are the opposite of over-centering. Whereas one may feel dissociated or sluggish if they remain in a centered state, one would become shallow and primitive if they stayed in a grounded state. Here are some signs of over-grounding:

- Skepticism/atheism
- Hedonistic living
- Over-ambition
- Money-loving/greed
- Lack of spiritual depth
- Religiosity
- Overeating
- Substance abuse/addiction

The above list notwithstanding, the world is more comfortable with people being over-grounded than over-centered. That's because the effects of over-grounding may still be compatible with living in the physical world. Some effects like over-ambition and greed may, in fact, be praised, and in many ways, are ingrained in the ethos of modern living. Whereas the reverse would probably be true on the astral plane: over-centered minds would be more adaptable and over-grounded minds would seem dysfunctional.

The antidote to over-grounding, of course, is centering, and a balance between the two is the very definition of actualized human existence. It is the proper way for your psychic self to live out the years of your incarnation effectively. It represents a balanced incarnation.

For now, if we gain the wisdom and skill to center and ground as needed, we will find happiness and fulfillment as creatures of the Divine Mind. We will live out our incarnations in reasonable contentment during the time allotted to us, and we will weather the lessons of life that are set before us. Unfortunately, however, there are forces that will prevent that if they can. There are negative spiritual forces in the world that can trip us up if we are not aware of them. And that is the subject of the next chapter.

Chapter 6

Shielding

---●●---

You are a Target

As soon as you start living as a self-realized psychic person, you will notice an increase in negative forces coming against you. This is to be expected. It happens to everyone in proportion to how spiritually oriented they become. What is needed is a way to defend ourselves from those spiritual forces that have the power to bring us down. *Shielding* is how we do that.

While there are many types of negative forces, most of them will fall into one of three types: unevolved spirits, psychic vampires, and skeptics.

These three entities employ negative forces for a variety of reasons, and they also attack each other and physical-first people as well, but they are especially attracted to the spiritual light radiating off psychic people. Therefore, you can expect to encounter them more often as you grow in psychic strength than you ever normally would.

An attack by a negative force drains the happiness created by spiritual awareness and practices. It's not that the unevolved spirit, the psychic vampire, or the skeptic want to diabolically stop you from being spiritual, rather they want to feed off what you have in one way or another. This feeding is what drains you, and eventually it will break you spiritually.

Sadly, if a negative force breaks your spiritual orientation, it will leave you unhappier than you ever were before you began trying to grow out of your physical-first life. Once that kind of unhappiness sets in, there's little chance of getting rid of it, because what got rid of it in the first place has been broken. A person then ends up in a kind of middle state where they want to be spiritually whole, but they can't find a way to do that. So, they are forever frustrated and discontent.

If you lacked peace and tranquility, then found it through psychic living, then lost it, you will have more discord than you ever had in the first place. It's like being poor: You can be happy and poor, but you can never be happy being poor if you used to be wealthy. So, if you find the spiritual light, and all the blessings therein, you must shield against the forces that seek to steal it from you. Shielding is as necessary to spirit-first living as the knowledge you gain about God or yourself, or the abilities you develop in centering and grounding.

Let's look at each of these negative-force entities in turn:

The Unevolved Spirit

The unevolved spirit is a person who has never grown out of their physical-first mode of living, but they're a little bit more than that.

It's natural in life to start out physical-first. Children are physical-first, animals are physical-first, but they don't drain your spirit. They are early spirits, not unevolved spirits. Their physical-first orientation is natural for where they are in life. They aren't diabolical because of it. Most of the time, they are dependent because of it, and in the case of children, hopefully will be growing out of it.

The unevolved spirit is different. It is physical-first and it actively resists spiritual growth. They resist spiritual growth because they are lazy, narcissistic, or both. And the keyword here is *resist*. They do not want to become psychic self-realized people. It's too much work, and they would have to admit that they are not as perfect as they already believe they are.

The result is that when they encounter a psychic person, they become hostile. They're either openly hostile, or they're passive-aggressive, or even sabotaging. The spiritual person painfully reminds them that they are not where they should be in their life. Thus, they are left with two choices: evolve or bring the spiritual person down to an unevolved state like they are. And this is the difference between an early spirit and an unevolved spirit.

Early spirits, such as children, are encouraged, inspired, and motivated by psychic people to evolve into psychic people themselves, they just never understood or saw an example they could follow. The unevolved spirit knows full well they should be spiritually oriented, but they are not inspired or encouraged. Rather, they are irritated and feel judged and condemned.

One would think they would want to be as far from the spiritual person as possible, but instead they actively seek them out to bring them down. They do this, because the one thing that makes them feel good again is to see the fall of an evolved spirit.

If a psychic person can be broken or brought back down to physical-first living, then the unevolved spirit feels justified. They no longer feel there's anything of substance that they are missing. They feel stronger and better than the spirit-person they cracked, so they feel good about their unevolved state. In other words: You are attractive to them, because they want to break you.

Here are the signs that you've encountered an unevolved spirit. The list is not exhaustive, but it includes the most common features:

Ten Signs of an Unevolved Spirit

1. They accuse you of thinking you're better than they are.

2. They belittle your beliefs.

3. They religiously oppose your beliefs.

4. They try to make you out to be superstitious.

5. They pick out your faults.

6. They talk behind your back to get others to agree with them.

7. They tempt you to act against your beliefs.

8. They treat you as if you were crazy.

9. They try to make you angry.

10. They openly ignore you or disrespect you.

Four Defenses Against an Unevolved Spirit

1. Recognize what they are.

If you are attacked by an unevolved spirit, the very first thing you must do is recognize it. As you can see from the list above, it is easy to think these attacks are your fault. You may find yourself searching endlessly and hopelessly for ways to modify your approach to that person or treat them differently or better.

You will always feel guilty for coming off wrong to them or wishing you hadn't told them this or that about yourself. You will eventually feel negative toward them or even bitter, but you will always come to the same conclusion that no matter how you try to rectify the relationship, the only way they will be happy is if you do not exist. When you come to that conclusion, and hopefully long before then, you must recognize you are being attacked.

2. Detach from them.

The next thing you must do with an unevolved spirit is to get away from it. If you cannot do this physically, perhaps because you work with them or live with them, then you must detach yourself from them in your mind. Do not share your beliefs with them. Leave them to their own misery, and consider what Jesus said about it: *Do not give dogs what is holy; and do not throw your pearls before swine, lest they trample them under foot and turn to attack you* (Matthew 7:6 RSV).

If you do throw your spirit-first pearls before an unevolved spirit, you will receive further confirmation of what they are. They will attack you in one way or another every time.

If possible, ignore them, even if it means being alone. It's better to be alone and psychically realized than to find your only company is an unevolved spirit. Find ways to be around other psychic people as much as you can. That is the best way to counter the effects of unevolved spirits.

3. Do not try to help.

This next step is very important: Realize that you cannot help an unevolved spirit. Realize what you are dealing with. They are not simply new spirits or innocently physical-first children as we all are at some point in our lives. They are actively physical-first; they know they shouldn't be, and they hate people who remind them of that, but they do not want to change. So, you must stop thinking that you can change them.

4. Do not succumb to them.

Do not give into whatever temptations they throw your way to move you toward physical-first living. Do not let exposure to their nature depress you and steal your light by imitating what they do. Do not let them be the moral influence that allows you to do things you have grown away from.

Remember, if they can get you to act like them, they will feel better about themselves, and you will feel worse about yourself, and that is their goal. So, however you can remove yourself from their presence and influence, do so.

Each tactic and attack of an unevolved spirit could be the subject of its own book, and we can't cover all possible attacks in this one, but take time to consider and even study the unevolved spirits you encounter. They are out there, because they are ubiquitous. Everyone has them in their life. Recognize them, identify their methods of attack, and find your own creative solutions. You are, after all, more enlightened than they are.

The Psychic Vampire

It may be possible to avoid an unevolved spirit, but a psychic vampire is a different spiritual species altogether. They are not necessarily physical-first people, and they are not jealous or angry that you are psychically spiritual. Rather, they seek you out specifically because you are psychic and proceed to psychically suck the positive energy from you.

The first feeling you may have for a psychic vampire is compassion. This is normal for spirit-people. After all, if someone is sad or down, or in need of a spiritual boost, we want to provide that to them. Many spirit-people get into the psychic arts with that very intention. But the psychic vampire doesn't want to be emotionally healed.

Psychic vampires are not really in need. They know enough about spirituality to feed themselves, but they choose to be a spiritual parasite and take spiritual nourishment from their host. They will work on the sparse energy they can get from regular people, but the light shining from the soul of the psychic person promises a rich and continuing meal for them. They will latch on to you immediately.

The prevailing characteristic of a psychic vampire is the need to make you feel sorry for them. They will catastrophize every aspect of their life so you are ever-increasingly pouring compassion towards them. They bask in that compassion—and they never give any back—never. Any exchange of compassion is a mere ruse to get more from you. Consider the following script. It is a typical example of a conversation with a psychic vampire:

Mary: Hello Sue, how's it going?

Sue: Well, he did it again?

Mary: Oh, really? What happened?

Sue: Bill comes in and tells me, I didn't wash the clothes he needs for work, and I told him, I can't do the laundry, get the kids ready for school, and take care of everything else that has to be done in the morning. I just need a little help, you know?

Mary: Sue, honey, I understand, that's not very fair at all.

Sue: Well, that's not all. He went out fishing the other day, and comes back, and he's bought all this new gear. I mean, he doesn't pay for it. I pay for it. It's my credit card, and he doesn't even ask me. And I'm breaking my back at this job, not that he cares at all.

Mary: That's terrible. Why doesn't he get a job?

Sue: Oh, he's had jobs, but I'm the one who's getting ill from all of this. I went to the doctor, and he says my thyroid is nearly non-functional. He says I have to go on medication.

Mary: You poor thing, Sue. I have that condition as well. When I was first diagnosed, I...

Sue: Well, it's not just that. They tell me my weight is causing problems with my back and knees. I'm in pain all the time, not that Bill cares or helps me with anything. I hurt all the time, but I still have to get the kids ready, make breakfast, come to work all day, and that's not all. My sister is splitting up from her husband. Did I tell you about that? He beats her. Bill's never hit me, but I think he could. I really do, and the stress of living with that fear is taking a toll. It's really taking a toll. Well, my sister and her four kids are coming to live with us, so I have that to deal with, but someone has to help, and as usual, I'm the helper. I help everyone.

Mary: Oh, no...

Sue: I have that, and my own kids and Bill, and he may not hit me yet, but he's so mentally abusive. Do you know what it's like to live with that?

And the script could go on and on, and if you're with a psychic vampire it does. If you work with them, they can go on all day. By the time, you've spent an hour listening to them, you feel depressed, lacking energy, cynical, and even worse, you feel your compassion fading. So, you stop listening, which you consider rude, but you don't know what else to do. You are sinking, and that's exactly how it feels.

But the psychic vampire knows how to deal with your silence. They lure you back in with a kind-of false compassion for you. The script goes like this:

Sue: *You're quiet today. I hope everything is alright. How's the baby?*

Mary: *(Surprised) Oh, fine. I just feel a bit tired. I was up late last night with the baby. I guess she has a cold.*

Sue: *My oldest had a cold, and I took her to the doctor, but they wouldn't do anything for her, so I had to take her to another ER, and do you think Bill would help? Nope. He just sat watching TV the whole time. Did I tell you he went out fishing the other day with his friend, and bought a hundred dollars' worth of new gear. On my credit card! So, I guess I just have to work some more hours now to make up for that, but if I don't take it easy, my back and knees are going to go out. Did I tell you they say I might need an operation in the future?*

Mary: *No, that sounds bad.*

Sue: *Well, that's not the worst of it. I now have to get up extra early to help my sister with her special needs child. As if I didn't have enough to do...*

And so, the script continues. The psychic vampire only shows enough interest in you to create a small compassion debt to get you listening, and then they start feeding off you again.

And why do they single you out? Because you'll listen. You are a spiritually sensitive person, so you have a higher degree of empathy than most people, and that means you are more willing to listen and take on the pain the vampire is dishing out. And here's the interesting part: Over time, you will feel worse about their situation than you do your own. You will spend more time caring about them than you do caring for yourself. You will begin to wither, because nothing will be coming back from them, and you're not a vampire yourself, so it is a net loss to you. You have nowhere to restore yourself. What's more, you will begin to feel worse about their situations than even they feel about it.

The danger here is the underlying cynicism that builds up within the spiritual person. At some point, you will have nothing left to give. The empathy within you will shut down. You may begin to feel a genuine hatred for the psychic vampire, but hide that hatred behind a mask of empathy. That dichotomy, that hypocrisy, will start to dim your spiritual orientation.

It's not uncommon to find the host of a psychic vampire seeking out pleasures from the world to compensate for the pain they are feeling from that connection. This may include over-eating, drug abuse, excessive smoking, or even more self-destructive behaviors like cutting behaviors, or even suicide attempts. The obvious psychiatric implications aside, this type of compensatory grounding behavior extinguishes any effects of centering. In short, your soul is broken; it is psychically sucked dry.

If you are going to be a psychic person, and enjoy the benefits of that spiritual evolution here and in the hereafter then you must learn how to protect yourself from psychic vampires, because they will find you. They will find you at work, at home, online, in school, and within any social circle you chose to move. Wherever it may be, they will find you. The light you shine will attract them.

To shield against a psychic vampire, the first thing you must do is learn to recognize them:

Thirteen Signs of a Psychic Vampire

1. They are always negative.

2. They are always a victim of something.

3. They are always a martyr.

4. They show little concern for your situations.

5. They tell you more information about their personal life than you ask for.

6. You feel manipulated into having compassion for them.

7. They demand more attention than anyone else.

8. They take no responsibility for their situation.

9. They never seem to take any steps to fix their situation.

10. They quickly become your friend by sharing their personal information with you.

11. You feel they are sticky, and you want to have a break from them.

12. You dread talking with them.

13. You feel drained or down after being around them.

Four Defenses against a psychic vampire

1. Control your compassion.

The first thing you must do is learn to shut down your compassion. As soon as you recognize that you are being sucked on by a psychic vampire, you must close down your compassion for them. Your compassion is not helping them, that is a deception. The only thing that can help is for them to step up and take control of their own life. But even that is a deception: They do have control, but they don't want their misery to go away. They want to inflict it on you.

Shutting down your compassion is not the same thing as hating someone. Hating someone is an active emotion you expend energy on toward the goal of hurting that other person. Shutting down compassion is just looking away. Stop saying to yourself in your mind, "How can I help this person?" Realize that you can't, and they don't want your help anyway.

You must understand that psychic people are typically empathic. That means that they have a psychic intuition of the feelings and emotions of others, and that intuition causes them to experience the emotions themselves. That doesn't mean you need to be empathic to be psychic. An empath is often not in control of their empathy. They can't help feeling what others are feeling. Self-realized psychic people should be in total control of their empathy and who they tune into.

Think about it: even Jesus didn't heal everyone in Israel. He only performed miracles on some of the people, not all of them. His reasoning is incidental; the fact is, he was in control of his compassion. He didn't take on the suffering of others, because to do so would have shut him down along with them. So, when it comes to a psychic vampire, when you realize that's what's latched onto you, you must control your compassion.

2. Be willing to end the relationship.

In the case of a psychic vampire, you must be willing to end your friendship with them. If they cannot suck from you, they will be cold to you. The truth is, sometimes the world is such a cold place that in our lives, if it weren't for the psychic vampires, we'd have no contact with anyone at all. This is a truly sad situation, but it is a fact of life.

It also is supported by the fundamental truth of centering which states that you are alone in the universe. The key is not to turn to the psychic vampires for company, but to seek out and find other spirit-people you can be around, and you must be willing to be alone until you find them.

3. Avoid the vampires.

Avoid being around a psychic vampire if you can. If you cannot, then actively negate what they are saying. Unfortunately, this may make you seem rude or uncaring, but it doesn't have to be ongoing, just enough to shut them down and let them know you're not a sucker (pun intended). Here is an example script of how it might go.

Sue: Well, that's not the worst of it. I now have to get up extra early to help my sister with her special needs child. As if I didn't have enough to do...

Mary: We all have crosses to bear, Sue. That's what families are for.

Of course, you won't be friends with Sue for very long after that, but part of defending yourself is accepting that you won't be friends with that person. But of course, you never really were; you were a host, and she was a vampire.

4. Contain the relationship.

Don't let the relationship get too far. If you can do nothing to defend yourself, at least contain the situation. If the vampire is a work colleague, then only be around them when you have to at work. Do not socialize with them in any other way. If they are a friend, do not be their lover. If they are a lover, do not move in with them, and if you have moved in with them, do not marry them. Do whatever you can to contain the situation.

Extricating ourselves from a psychic vampire relationship can be difficult. Especially if they are already ingrained into our lives. If your mother or father is a psychic vampire, it can be hard to defend yourself against that, but there are still things you can do. Don't live at home. Remind yourself that you don't have to "feel" bad for them, even if you feel obligated to help them. Practice centering and grounding in the right measures, and try to find time for yourself. Remember: You have your own troubles in life; you don't have to feel their pain.

The Skeptic

To be skeptical means to doubt. It means that you demand proof before you will accept something as true. It means the scientific method of thinking is better than superstition. And all that sounds very good and logical, and it would be if that's where skepticism stopped, but it doesn't; it becomes malignant, and when it does, it doesn't just kill superstition, it kills our ability to have hope as well, and when we lose hope, we eventually sink into despair.

Skepticism is a negative force that has spiritually ruined more people than just about any other effect from any other source. It seeps in and is so pervasive that almost everyone in the modern world has become skeptical to some degree.

It's not about truth.

But understand that at the root of skepticism is not a reverence for the truth, but rather a kind of mental laziness. It's a refusal to look beyond the physical world, because the physical world is what's easy to see and figure out. It's a refusal to examine the intuitive aspects of one's mind or to figure out the implications of psychic phenomena.

Skeptics find it easier just to doubt anything other than what they can see, hear, feel, smell, and taste. Thus, the result of skepticism is a return to physical-first thinking and living.

Even when a skeptic experiences something paranormal, they simply doubt it. If they have a precognitive dream for instance, which is a common experience among many people, they just ignore it. They consider it a coincidence and disregard it. They are spiritually lazy in that way, and it's easier for them to forget about a mysterious dream that showed them a future event than to examine the implications of it.

After all, if they were to believe they had seen the future directly or symbolically in a dream, then they would have to admit the mind cannot be generated from the brain, because there just isn't anything neurologically that would allow for a mental vision of an event that has not yet happened.

But if they accept the mind is separate from the brain, then they would also have to conclude that death doesn't affect the mind. And if death won't affect the mind, then it might lead to asking what they are doing in this world in the first place?

And if they ask that question, they might have to ask themselves what good it is to live as a spirit in the physical world, and why were they created in the first place, and by whom or what? All that spiritual work would take them over a cliff they might never be able to climb back up. It might overwhelm them, and it might change them, and they don't want to be changed.

So, accepting a dream as precognitive foreshadows a great deal of spiritual work and introspection, and the skeptic simply doesn't want to go there. It's too exhausting and just a lot easier to simply doubt it. And when they doubt, they immediately find a great deal of support for their skepticism from a physical-first world that readily accepts them for who they are.

The world revolves on skepticism. Skepticism has seeped into the most powerful institutions within civilization. The scientific community, of course, is utterly skeptical, but so too is the legal system, and the medical establishment. Even government, an institution that in the past was founded and authorized by religious faith, is now entirely taken over by skepticism.

So, you as a spiritual/psychic person will encounter skepticism not only from the person at work, but pervasively throughout every day of your life. And just like a disease, it can take hold in you if you are not mindful of it and careful in your spiritual hygiene.

Scientific Thought vs. Skepticism

Scientific thinking is good. Put simply, with scientific thinking you make an observation, you form a hypothesis (a proposed reason) to explain that observation, you test your hypothesis through experimentation that will either prove or disprove it. If the hypothesis is proved correct, you have your explanation for the observation, and that forms your belief about it. If it's disproved, you form another hypothesis, and continue experimenting until you find an explanation for the observation.

No one can argue with the scientific way of reasoning. Scientific thinking is used to develop knowledge about the world, but it can just as easily be used in philosophy, spirituality, and it even applies to the astral plane. It is the proper way to think about things.

The opposite of scientific thinking is superstition. Superstitious thinking takes an observation and goes straight to a belief about it. And the belief is uneducated. It's uneducated because no mental effort has gone into forming a hypothesis, and no experimentation has been done to prove the hypothesis one way or another.

In the world today, superstition is rife. It is what replaces knowledge in the mind of the ignorant and mentally lazy. Superstitious thinking is not good. We should be more discerning and critical in our thinking. That's why the Divine Mind made us the way he did. He gave us the mental capability to find the truth in all things. He gave us, as the only animal on earth to have it, the ability for scientific thought.

But skepticism is not scientific thought. Skepticism is really the dark sibling of superstition. Skepticism refuses to make the observation in the first place, and thus goes straight to disbelief.

The problem is that in a physical-first world skeptical thinking is more palatable than superstition. Remember, the institutions of civilization have become entirely skeptical, so if you are not a skeptic as well, you are considered superstitious. And if you are viewed as superstitious, you are cast down into a pit with all the, ignorant, primitive, bestial people.

Even a belief in God, while perhaps tolerated because so many people believe in God, is seen by the skeptical elite as a holdover of superstition. A belief in psychic phenomena is laughed at and denied entirely, even though billions of people have experienced it. Consciousness apart from the brain is considered a belief in magic, even though it is clearly proved scientifically as we discussed in the chapter on the mind. Religion of any sort is laughed at, especially if one holds to any sort of notion that the bio-logical evolution of species had any Divine direction.

In fact, when it comes to any unexplained phenomena, skepticism would rather have us be ignorant than to be-lieve any theory that is not skepticism-approved.

So, when you tell a skeptic that you travel to the astral plane in your mind, or have ascended for brief moments into the Mind of God through centering meditation, you will not be taken seriously. Even if they don't openly pat-ronize you, they will ignore you. You cannot be one of them and say things like that. And don't forget, they hold the reigns of the most powerful institutions in civilization. So, how long can your spiritual orientation withstand that?

Skeptics come at you from everywhere, and the ap-proach can be insidious. The goal of skepticism is to con-vince you that anything spiritual is impossible, and that to believe in any spiritual ideas, or to even entertain them as a possibility, puts you into a lower order of mental evolu-tion.

Unfortunately, in this world, over time, skeptics are winning. It is so pervasive in schools, colleges, and in popular science that If you asked most people to point to their mind, they would automatically point to their head.

They wouldn't point up or try to explain it in any oth-er way. Most people believe the mind comes from the brain, and they believe that because skeptics over time have worked very hard to convince them that they are nothing more than physical accidents of evolution in a world and universe that is itself nothing more than an accident.

They have worked hard to convince the masses there is no spirit, no Divine Mind, no life other than what they can hear, see, feel, taste, or smell. You must counter this influence in your own life or it will erode your psychic self-realization.

Three Ways to Counter the Effects of Skepticism

There are three things you can do to counter the effects of skepticism in your life. They are simple, and if you stick to them, you will not experience skepticism's corrosive effects.

1. Be skeptical of skepticism.

Fight fire with fire. Skepticism, once you start to see it, seems as if it's desperate to reinforce its dogma. So, be very careful what you accept as true, or expert, or scientific.

When you hear statements like, "Through evolution, the human brain has come to sense itself." Be skeptical of that. Doubt it first and make them prove their point before you believe it or just blindly accept it.

Just because something is stated by a Ph.D. who is the head of some department, and you feel that makes them smarter than you, don't believe it. Because they don't know. Most of the time they're just pretending they do. They're just repeating what someone else has told them and that they have blindly accepted themselves.

This may require you to do some research and gain some understanding on your own. But it's easier now than it's ever been to be self-educated. Remember, the journal article on training paramecium is not in the textbooks used in schools. But it is online now. And there's lots of information online and in books that's more available now than it ever was before.

Of course, I realize this is easier for some people to do than others. Skepticism runs so deep and is so repeated it can be inescapable. I recently read an article in a new age, spiritual, magazine, and the author of the article was explaining psychic mental phenomena in terms of biochemical and psychological processes of the brain. The fact that the brain can't make the mind, and psychology applies only to the mind, and psychic phenomena completely upturns current theories of consciousness, was lost on this "spiritual" author—the author had bought in completely to the skeptical hype of brain-equals-consciousness.

And in truth, it does take a lot of self-education in science and philosophy to see past the hype. Not everyone is trained to do that. But here are some facts that will keep you skeptical of skepticism:

- Telepathy in humans and animals has been scientifically documented.

- Precognition in dreams is scientifically documented.

- Paramecium can be trained, and that has been scientifically documented.

- Conscious observation of subatomic particles affects their behavior, and that has been scientifically documented.

No matter what the credentials are of any scientist or author you may come across, if they can't fit those facts into their theory of how the brain creates the mind, then they are only spouting a skeptical belief, not a fact, and when it comes to beliefs, your beliefs are just as valid as theirs. So, be very skeptical of skepticism.

2. Ask simple questions.

It's amazing how simple these deeper questions can be. When an atheist says, "There is no god." Just ask, "How do you know?" Their logic will start to fall apart.

When they respond, "Because no one has ever seen God?" Just ask, "How could something like God be seen with eyeballs?"

When someone says, "The brain generates the mind." Just ask, "Really? How does it do that?"

They will say, "Through the activity of billions of neurons in your brain." Then ask, "What activity? How does that work?" They won't be able to answer. It is a well-known fact that we have no clue why anyone is conscious or even why consciousness exists in the first place. Nothing explains it. And yet, it is the most common phenomena in the world.

So, when someone says, "We evolved into what we are, no God is needed for that." Just ask, "Why does evolution work? Why does the universe even work according to evolution?" Then they will say, "We don't know, but science will one day explain it." And then you'll realize you're dealing with atheistic faith, not fact.

Just stick with simple, innocent questions and skepticism will crumble at your feet, because in the end, physical-first people don't know as much as they pretend to know.

The important things of this universe are mysteries. What is gravity? Why does it exist? How can a photon of light be both a particle and a wave at the same time? Because that's a contradiction. Who is perceiving red when the nerves in my eyeballs send signals to nerves in my brain? Neither my eyeballs nor the nerves in my brain are conscious? So, who or what is "seeing" red? The fact is simple questions crumble physical-first skepticism.

3. Associate with psychic people.

Perhaps the best way to counter the effect of skepticism in your life is to actively choose to associate with psychic people. You must understand that your spiritual orientation is for you in this life. You don't have to convert anyone to your beliefs, so don't fight with skeptics. Let them have their world. Seek out others like yourself in your 3D world or online, and associate with them. Spend your time with them.

The things you know, the things you have experienced, all the wonders you've been shown through meditation and psychic practice are invisible to skeptics. Might as well keep it that way.

Unit Three

Your Psychic Art

———————•●•———————

Once you have the basic knowledge and skills for developing your psychic self, you need to pick a psychic art. Just as there are many psychological aspects of mind, there are many parapsychological aspects of mind as well. Practicing the psychic arts connects humans to the spiritual world while at the same time providing advantages in the physical world.

Moreover, it provides a balance between the two aspects of mind, and that means greater mental health. Think of practicing the psychic arts as a kind of therapy you can do for yourself. If you practice an art in which you are naturally gifted, you're naturally going to become a happier person.

Keep in mind, while there is no prohibition against it, there's also no requirement that one become a public, private, or professional psychic. No one has to perform their psychic art for anyone other than themselves. What matters is that a spiritual person maintains their connection to the psychic aspects of mind, so they can fully function as self-realized psychic people.

We are going to examine three broad categories of the psychic arts. Almost all the psychic arts fall into one of these archetypes. As you read them, you will no doubt discover an attraction, an inkling you feel, or maybe even some experience you've had in one of them.

We will look at the astrologer, the medium, and the witch, and we'll break down the categories and give insight as to how you can determine if that's the right psychic art for you. Then we'll look at some tips on how to get started. So, let's begin our exploration.

Chapter 7

The Astrologer

———————●●———————

Picture yourself on a hill near a river watching the night sky when there are no lights from any city or car. It's 3000 B.C. somewhere in Ancient Mesopotamia. (Today that would be the area of Iran, Iraq, Syria, and Kuwait.) The only light you have are the dying embers of a campfire lit earlier in the day. The sheep you herd, and the dogs that help you herd them, have all laid down for the night. It's just you awake and watching.

You'd normally be reclining in your tent, but for some reason you're not tired. There are no books, computers, or phones to occupy your attention, so it's silent except for a warm breeze and the sounds of the Tigris river off in the distance. You're happy for the weather that is on your side for once, and you consider it a run of good luck.

Above you in the sky are lights of unimaginable mystery. You have no idea what they are or why they are there.

You've been staring at them every night for years, and you noticed a long time ago that the same patterns of stars move across the sky every night, from the eastern horizon to the western one.

Some of these patterns remind you of animals and objects and you give them names like Leo, Scorpio, and Libra, and you happen to notice throughout the year that these constellations never change, yet there are bright wandering stars that travel through them, and even the moon travels through them the same way over the course of a month.

When the sun comes up in the morning, it outshines all the stars, and throughout the year it comes up in one of twelve different star patterns you've named throughout your life as a rancher. This month the pattern you call The Virgin is on the eastern horizon when the sun comes up. It's just after the harvest, and the temperature is finally cooling off.

On a night like this, you're not at all surprised to see a bright wandering star moving through one of the patterns that looks like a figure with a bow and arrow; you call it Sagittarius. Whenever it moves through Sagittarius, good luck seems to be with you and the sheep. If you can, you wait for that alignment of the star and Sagittarius before you move the sheep from your northern fields to your southern farm. It's not always possible, but when it is, it's worth the wait.

Eventually, your children grow older and enter the sheep-herding trade. You teach them about the stars, and the wanderers that you can see at night, and you even make a chart so the stars can be tracked and described.

Eventually, you make several scrolls describing what you've learned, and these scrolls you leave to your children.

Later generations notice that when a certain bright wandering star (Jupiter) enters the star pattern that looks like a bull (Taurus), a better price is had on the sale of sheep. It's a better price for sure than when another wandering star (Saturn) enters that same star pattern. So, they make note of it, and no one tries to sell sheep if they can avoid it when Saturn is in Taurus.

All that information keeps getting added to, and it keeps getting passed down from generation to generation. The predictions become more precise, and the ancient people come to rely on them. They just assume that God made the heavens in such a mechanical way so they can know the future and make decisions based on that knowledge. What other reason could there be for all the little lights in the sky?

————————

Thus, astrology is born. It relies on the symbols of nature in the heavens to predict what will happen in the future, or at least to explain why things are the way they are at certain times. In the hands of a skilled astrologer, an astrological horoscope can provide a wealth of information.

For thousands of years, kings and queens employed astrologers to examine the heavens, to make charts, and answer the questions they wanted to know about. Today, we think astrology has gone the way of bronze age sheep herders. Surely, it's been replaced by the science of astronomy, cosmology, and astrophysics.

But ask anyone anywhere in the Western World what their birth sign is, and they will know it. The *Farmer's Almanac*, based on agricultural astrology, has been published for 200 years, and is still sold in bookstores and grocery stores all over America. Not to mention Nancy Reagan, the wife of President Ronald Reagan, regularly consulted an astrologer, Joan Quigley, to plan her husband's schedule during his time in office.

The reason astrology endures is because it interprets symbols, symbols that are still meaningful to us today. A symbol is an object or occurrence that over time has come to stand for something else. The two things are correlated. For example, a scale means equality or fairness. The constellation of Aries means action, will, and maybe even war.

And the world is full of symbols. In the mid-eighteenth century (1749–1756), a Christian mystic, named Emanuel Swedenborg, coined the concept of *Correspondence* in his *Arcana Coelestia*. By that he meant that everything we experience in the physical world is a symbol, a communication from God, because, as he puts it, the universe came from God and contains his image. The idea being that we can derive all truth about nature from the symbols we find in nature.

Astrologer-types are all about the symbols that are found in nature. An astrologer-type sees communications in the way nature presents itself. An astrologer is someone who believes the Divine Mind communicates to us through the symbols we find all around us every day.

One person may see a billboard on the side of the road, and to them it's just an advertisement. An astrologer-type sees the same billboard and ponders why they are seeing that message at that instance in time. On the surface it's an ad, but deeper down it could have been any ad; yet for some reason, it's an ad at that place on the highway intended to be seen by the astrologer as he or she passes by. So, they ponder it.

And when they ponder it, the psychic aspects of their mind start to kick in, especially the psychic ability of clairvoyance. Clairvoyance is the ability to see and know things that are not presented to the mind by any physical stimuli. With clairvoyance, we mentally sense the past, present, and future, and when the astrologer experiences clairvoyance upon seeing a symbol, they perceive its hidden meaning.

From that hidden meaning, they can give advice, predict the future, relay messages from the Divine, describe a person or thing as it really is, and even tell what potential lies within that person.

The main psychic arts of the astrologer-type include astrology, tarot divination, and dream interpretation. Granted there are many others; in fact, there are hundreds. Because any system of divination, aside from giving direct prophecies to people, typically relies on symbol interpretation. But the ones above are the most frequently encountered and the ones that symbol interpreters would most likely practice. So, for the sake of space in this book, we will confine our examination to them.

The reason why this archetype is called *The Astrologer* is that just about any form of psychic symbol-interpretation uses the language of astrology. Tarot, for instance, is considered a sister art of astrology, because nearly every card in a standard Rider-Waite deck has some astrological symbolism on it. The symbols found in astrology are so ancient that they've become ubiquitous in most symbolic psychic systems. Palmistry, for instance, relies heavily on astrological interpretations. Even in my own practice of dream interpretation, I have found that the transiting planets in a person's astrological birth chart often reflect the dream they are reporting.

So, let's look at each one of these in turn. As I describe them, ask yourself if that psychic art seems to fit with your personality and interests.

Astrology

Astrology considers the placement of planets and star constellations in the heavens at the time of someone's birth. It has been around some 25,000 years, and even its modern form is over 5000 years old. It is older than any religious system in the world. In Christianity, for instance, it was astrologers (Magi) who found the infant Jesus.

There are lots of subcategories of astrology. Some systems deal with events in the world (mundane astrology), some deal with elections (election astrology), some with finance, some with missing objects, some with places or events, but the one most people are concerned with is natal astrology. Natal (birth) astrology is the study of a person's individual horoscope, also known as their natal chart or birth chart.

A natal horoscope is simply a circle drawn on paper or by a computer, and is divided into twelve equal sections called houses. A circle has 360 degrees, so each house takes up thirty degrees of the circle. The earth is at the center of the circle, and the twelve star constellations of astrology (also called, the zodiac) rotate around the outside of the circle going past each of the 12 houses (one house every two hours). The constellations are called Aries, Taurus, Gemini, Cancer, Leo, Virgo, Libra, Scorpio, Sagittarius, Capricorn, Aquarius, and Pisces.

The planets also travel around the circle. Some take a brief time to travel the whole circle. (The moon takes only one month.) Some take a long time (Pluto is 248 years.) The sun takes exactly one year.

When a person is born, depending on where they are on earth, and at what day and time they were born, the constellations and planets will be at a specific location on that birth chart. What everyone knows is where the sun was, and that's called a person's sun sign. I was born on September 22, so my natal sun was in Virgo. Thus, I am a Virgo.

All the constellation positions and planetary positions can be looked up and calculated from a big book called an ephemeris. But no one does that anymore. Today, everyone just uses a computer with an astrological program. You can even go on the internet and get your birth chart done for free at www.astro.com. Of course, if you want it interpreted for you, you must pay.

Every constellation, planet, and house has a symbolic meaning. An astrologer looks at the chart and analyzes it. For instance, what does it mean that a person's third house is dominated by Scorpio, or what does it mean that Neptune is in the eighth house which is dominated equally by Virgo and Libra? If the sun represents life energy, and it is in Virgo in the tenth house, what does that tell us about a person's primary drive in life?

Thus, astrologers are scientific-minded people. They like to study astronomy; they tend to be mathematically inclined, and they enjoy analyzing things. They are also inclined toward psychology and psychiatry. The famous psychiatrist, Carl Jung, was a proponent of astrology.

If one learns it on a basic level, Astrology is not hard to learn, but astrology can become very involved and has great depth. Geometry and trigonometry are the math involved in astrology. And one must be somewhat academically inclined to delve beyond the surface and really understand it.

For instance, it's one thing to know that Jupiter means good fortune. It's another thing to study the ancient Roman god, Jupiter, and understand why he became a symbol for that. Or to study the physical nature of the planets themselves, astronomically, to understand the underlying reasons for the symbolism they are given.

Math, history, analysis, and research are skills of the advanced astrologer. Stargazing, of course, with or without a telescope is the preferred hobby of the astrologer. It's one thing to see the planets on a computer-generated chart, it's another thing to behold their symbolic significance in the real night sky.

So, is astrology for you? Maybe you should start by having your birth chart analyzed by an astrologer and see how you feel about it.

Tarot

Tarot is a system of divination using tarot cards. The word *divination* means reading the future, particularly by receiving a message from the Divine Mind. So, tarot is actually a form of prophecy. With tarot, the divination is accomplished by shuffling the deck, dealing out a number of cards in a prescribed manner (the *spread*), and then interpreting what those cards mean.

Like all forms of *cartomancy* (telling the future with cards), the idea is that God will control your hands while you are shuffling and dealing the cards, and the resulting spread, will be the message the person (called a sitter) is supposed to receive. Essentially, God gives order to the random shuffling of the cards the same way he gives order to the orbiting planets and stars in astrology.

Some people believe the tarot cards are very old. Some believe they only came to the fore in the early 20th century. Both theories are correct.

The standard tarot cards we use today, the Rider-Waite deck, was created in 1910. However, cartomancy, that is telling the future with playing cards, stretches back centuries.

The imagery of the Rider-Waite deck is also centuries old, but the symbolism of those images, especially those of the Major Arcana (the first section of the tarot deck) stretch back even further, thousands of years in fact, and they owe a great deal to astrology, Ancient Egyptian mysticism, and Ancient Hebrew Kabbalah. Thus, some would say the symbolism of tarot is as old as the collective unconsciousness of mankind itself. The Rider-Waite tarot deck of 1910 merely displays those symbols.

The earliest tarot cards that are still in existence date back to 1392 AD. It is called the Gringonneur deck and was owned by Charles VI of France. There are only seventeen of them left. And though the location is still somewhat controversial, the Gringonneur deck is thought to be located in the Bibliotheque Nationale, in Paris.

Tarot Symbolism

A tarot deck consists of seventy-eight cards in two parts: a major arcana and a minor arcana. The word *arcana* means "secrets" or "mysteries." In the case of the tarot, it refers to the secret symbolism they contain. It's possible to do a reading with just one or the other, but usually readings are done with both arcanas intermingled.

The major arcana is a set of twenty-two cards with names like, The Fool, The Hierophant, The High Priestess, and the Emperor. The Minor Arcana, on the other hand, consists of fifty-six cards in four suits, with fourteen cards in each suit. The suits include: Wands, Pentacles, Cups, and Swords.

Like the planets, signs, and houses in astrology, each tarot card has an historical meaning attached to it. When the tarotist performs their shuffling ritual (which is unique to them) and lays down a spread they might see that The Fool card, meaning a journey, is next to the Five of Wands, meaning strife and competition, and conclude that an upcoming trip might be quite troublesome.

Unlike, astrology, tarot doesn't involve math. You don't need computers. You don't need someone to pull their birth certificate out to see what time they were born. The standard meanings of the cards are in many books and websites, and anyone can learn basic tarot if they want to, but the psychic sensitivity to the message is what really counts. Can the would-be tarotist decipher the true meaning of the cards? Can they tell what the psychic story is? Do they have faith that the Divine will control their hands while they shuffle the deck?

One way you can tell if tarot is for you is to simply get a deck of tarot cards, and before learning anything about them, ask the Divine a question in your mind, shuffle the cards thoroughly, and lay down the first three off the top of the deck. What do you see in the cards? If you look at the cards and all you see in them is chaotic chance occurrences that mean nothing, then tarot is not for you. On the other hand, if you feel there is a message there, if you see something in the cards, then perhaps you have the gift.

Again, you don't have to know anything about the cards. Just ask yourself if they feel positive. Or do they feel negative to you? Most importantly, do you believe you have received a message? Faith that you are receiving a message is the most important thing. If you then want to learn more about them, that's when you know tarot is for you.

Dream Interpretation

According to the National Sleep Foundation, even now in the twenty-first century, we have no idea why we dream.

There are certainly theories: One is that we do it to consolidate long-term memories; another is that we work out psychological problems, another is that we dream to reset neurotransmitter levels in the brain. But for one reason or another, all theories fall short of an explanation, or they are based on one observation about dreams only to be contradicted by another. Nothing explains why dreams are the way they are.

In dreams, we see people and places we've never seen before. We put together worlds we could never invent with our ordinary waking minds, and we experience events that have nothing to do with our normal lives.

Even more strange is that we often have a different mind as the person in our dream than we do when we are awake. It doesn't even dawn on us most of the time that we are in a dream, and when we wake up, as that mind fades, so too does the memory of the dream.

And that's all assuming the dream isn't precognitive. A precognitive dream is one that comes true. Seeing future events in a dream is a common experience. Many people have had astonishing precognition while dreaming. I once dreamed I saw ultralight airplanes flying around me. That very day, when I was going to work, I came over a hill and saw several ultralight airplanes flying around the valley below me. I had never seen them there before. I never saw them there again after that. The odds of that dream happening on that day is beyond any chance occurrence. I saw the future in my dream. And many people have had similar experiences.

A History of Dream Interpreting

Because of this, since ancient times, people have sought to interpret their dreams. You're probably aware of the story of Joseph in the book of Genesis in the Bible. The Egyptian Pharaoh had a dream that troubled him, and the only person who could tell him what the symbols meant (withered grain and starving cows) was Joseph. Because of that, Egypt was saved from a famine, and Joseph was promoted to an exalted position by the Pharaoh.

In Ancient Greece, in the city of Delphi, there was a temple called the Temple of Apollo. In that temple lived the Pythia. The Pythia was a High Priestess, and the person who held that position (always a female), was also called the Oracle of Delphi. If a pilgrim to the temple gave a sufficient offering, she would go into a dream trance, perhaps drug-induced, and begin to speak in cryptic messages that were later interpreted.

For over a thousand years, the institution of the Temple of Apollo and the Oracle of Delphi endured. Great matters of state were put to the Pythia for predictions, and people from all over came to have their futures divined by her. What she reported from her dream states could determine the course of everything from when a farmer planted his fields, to when an empire would declare war.

How I Got Into Dreams

So, even if we haven't figured out why we dream, one reason seems to have stood the test of time, and that's to receive messages from Divine Mind. In fact, when I first began my journey into the psychic arts, I began by interpreting dreams.

One night, in the fall of 2008, I had a lucid dream (a dream where you know you are dreaming and can control the dream to some degree), and I became interested in how I could induce lucid dreams at will. I searched the internet and stumbled across a forum called Dream Views. This was a forum where people would post a dream and ask others to interpret it. I read a few of the dreams, and it turned out I had a real knack for understanding the symbolism.

And it wasn't psychological symbolism. A lot of the members of the forum struggled to find psychological reasons for the dream images, but I saw in many of them a spiritual message. Sometimes, the messages I saw in the dreams were important messages that anyone could use, and thus the dream was more important to the group than even to the individual who had the dream.

For example, one member reported a dream where they were in an old house and felt in danger, and as they walked down into the basement, they encountered a ghost. It frightened them, so they ran back upstairs.

One interpreter said the dreamer was feeling psychological stress about moving into a new house, but I saw it differently. Of course, the dream could mean stress or anxiety, and probably did on some psychological level, but this person felt the dream had a deeper significance than the surface psychology, and I agreed.

I saw the house as representing the dreamer's soul, because a house contains them as a home, and their soul contains their life as a home. The dreamer was regressing in spiritual development (walking down stairs in an old house), or they were in danger of it. As they entered the basement, they viewed a dead person (the ghost), and this represented an earlier spiritual version of themselves, a version they had already grown out of. They sensed that the basement was a bad place and saw that it was full of death, so they ran back up the stairs; that is, they ascended back to where they were.

So, I told the member the dream was a warning for them not to regress in their spiritual development but to continue going higher. That was the message of the dream.

Dreams, without a doubt, are the number one way the Divine communicates with people. Everyone dreams, sometimes three or four times a night. Everyone has dreams they feel are significant; those dreams should be interpreted for their message.

It can be difficult to interpret our own dreams, because we are biased toward making them say what we want them to say. But an outsider with a gift for seeing the symbolic message behind the dream can offer a more accurate perspective.

Are you a dream interpreter? Usually, a good dream interpreter has an active dream life themselves. They have frequent dreams, and they have strange dreams. They tend to be creative types, but they love analysis as well. They become driven to know what the symbolic images mean, and when they read a dream someone else has had, they begin to see things in it. They begin to see a coherent symbolic message.

One way to find out if you're good at dream interpretation is to simply do what I did: visit a dream interpretation forum and try it out. Of course, Facebook Groups have pretty much taken over most internet forums, so you may want to search "dream interpretation" in the groups on Facebook.

At any rate, we've explored symbols and divination in this chapter, but what if symbolic analysis isn't your thing? What if astrology, tarot, and dreams don't really turn you on in a psychic way? Maybe you're more of an intuitive person, more in contact with vibrations and emotions than calculating planetary orbits or studying ancient symbols on cards. In that case, perhaps you're not an astrologer-type; maybe you're a medium. Find out in the next chapter.

Chapter 8

The Medium

———————— • ————————

The séance has been planned for over a month, and they've sent a carriage for you. The family already paid five pounds with five more guaranteed if they're satisfied with your work. That's a lot of money in 1870, especially for a middle-aged minister of a tiny Spiritualist church on the outskirts of London.

But Spiritualism has become very popular of late, and you gravitated to it because of your gift, a gift the upper class of London are more than happy to pay you for if you're willing to use that gift for them, and you are willing. In fact, your reputation for channeling is growing.

You know the sorrow of losing someone you love can last a lifetime, and you feel sympathy for the grieving people who come to your services for a chance to reconnect with their departed. You've felt the sting of it yourself, when the only man you ever loved was lost at sea decades ago. But you also know the dead are never far away.

After all, you hear them. Sometimes you see them. Sometimes you speak to them. Either way, the lost ones, their spirits, are always around you. They center on you in hopes of reaching those they've left behind.

So, you think of yourself as a bridge between two worlds: the world of the living, and the world of the dead. The spirits call to you, because you know they are still alive. They know they can communicate with you and through you, and you're their passageway back to the land of the living.

When you were young, your family thought you were odd, a bit left of center. You were always talking to imaginary friends, even when you got older. Your father worried if you didn't stop, you'd never find a husband. So, he put his foot down and said, "No more! Not in my house."

So, you stopped talking to them openly, but that didn't stop you from seeing them. Once at a party hosted by your father's employer, you followed a soldier into a drawing room. But when you walked in, the room was empty except for a painting of the man you followed hanging on the wall between the bookcases. You said nothing to anyone about that.

Now, the driver of the carriage helps you out and shows you to the front door. He knocks on it for you, and the matron of the manor invites you in and gushes with enthusiasm at your arrival. She shows you into her parlor where they have set everything up just as you requested.

There are chairs around a large Cherrywood table, and a single candle in the middle of it. When everyone is seated, the shades are drawn, the candle is lit, and you begin the séance, just as you have a hundred times before.

Mediumship is speaking with the so-called dead. That is, it is speaking with spiritual entities that are no longer operating in the physical world. There is evidence that the activity of communicating with the dead goes back some 28,000 years. Cave paintings by indigenous Australians date back that far and depict skulls, bones, spirits, and the afterlife.

In the book of 1 Samuel, in the Old Testament of the Bible, a rather extended passage of the Medium of Endor relates a séance with Saul where she brought up the departed Samuel to advise him. The book of Samuel, and that story, was written some 2,600 years ago. So, mediumship is clearly a very old psychic art.

There are three primary types of mediums: channeling mediums, physical mediums, and spiritual mediums. Then there are what I call the astral mediums. Let's look at each, then we'll look at some of the tools of mediumship, and then I have some advice for you if you think you might be a medium-type of psychic.

The Channeling Medium

A channeling medium channels the spirit through themselves into the physical world. This is done by allowing the spirit being contacted to possess their body and speak through them.

In this way, the sitter (the one getting the reading) talks directly to the departed using the medium as a kind-of psychic telephone. The medium will often speak in an altered voice as the spirit possesses them and takes control of their body. Sometimes they incorporate automatic writing or a talking board (which is explained below).

The Physical Medium

This form of mediumship uses physical phenomenon to send a message to the living world. These phenomena may include table tipping, various noises, things may levitate, smoke may be seen, or even ectoplasm.

Ectoplasm is a supernatural substance that comes out of the body of a medium, usually from their mouth, during a spiritualistic trance. It is supposed to allow the spirit entity to form a body in the physical world.

It's not uncommon for the medium to ask the spirit to give some sign that they are present in the séance. They will ask for a candle to flicker or a table to rattle, or a breeze to blow, any physical sign that they are present.

You don't encounter this kind of mediumship very often in the modern world. It was much more practiced in the nineteenth century. One reason is that many people are simply frightened of that form of séance. Another reason is that, unfortunately, many fraudulent psychics have used stage magic tricks to give the appearance of physical mediumship.

Thus, today, there is a great deal of skepticism that surrounds physical mediumship. Modern mediums, not wanting to be tainted with the fraud of the past, have avoided it. So, it has fallen mostly into disuse.

The Spiritual Medium

The spiritual medium relies on the psychic talent of clairvoyance. Clairvoyance is a general psychic term that can mean any kind of ESP (extrasensory perception) whereby a psychic receives information from spiritual or non-physical means. So, in the case of the medium, he or she can hear spiritual messages, see spiritual beings, or know things in their mind that the spirits communicate to them telepathically.

Spiritual mediumship is by far the most common mediumship practiced today. It doesn't require spirit possession like channeling does, and it isn't as impersonal as physical mediumship. It's not scary to witness, and it can incorporate the caring personality of the psychic who is doing the reading; that alone gives it many advantages.

A spiritual medium may tune in to the departed by holding an object of theirs or looking at a picture. They will typically ask the sitter questions about things that they are seeing, hearing or sensing. The sitter will either confirm or deny the information which helps the medium focus on the spiritual entity. It might play out something like the following script:

Medium: I see Robert with a red convertible. Does that mean anything to you?

Sitter: No, but he drove a red truck.

Medium: Yes, and did it have black seats?

Sitter: No, they were brown, but he had them covered with black seat covers.

Medium: I also see a woman with him, more like a young girl perhaps. It is someone he is close to.

Sitter: Yes, his sister died when she was young.

As the medium reports things and asks questions, he or she gains a more precise focus. They may take questions from the sitter and sense any replies telepathically from the departed and report those back. And so, the session would go for whatever length of time was agreed upon or until the medium falls out of contact with the departed.

Again, this is the most popular type of mediumship. It is also the type that is practiced in most Spiritualist churches, and by the popular television mediums like John Edward or Theresa Caputo.

The Astral Medium

Finally, there is a debatable form of mediumship. It's debatable in that some psychics don't consider it mediumship at all. The technique relies on astral travel and remote viewing, but whereas remote viewing usually involves viewing a physical location, in astral mediumship, the remote viewing takes place on the astral plane.

Typically, the medium enters a trance state and then projects their mind into the astral plane to find the departed. Once the departed is found, the medium reports back what they have seen. They may even try to contact the spirit and form a telepathic bond whereby they can channel information back and forth.

Astral mediumship is like spiritual mediumship, but it doesn't rely on the spirit contacting the medium. Theoretically, therefore, anyone who has crossed over could be found and reported on.

In channeling, physical, and spiritual mediumship, the departed comes to the medium and wants to make contact. With astral mediumship, the departed is found whether they wanted to be found or not.

A significant drawback with astral mediumship is that spirits may be found who are unwilling to communicate or want nothing to do with the sitter or with memories of their past life. The medium would then have a responsibility to tell the sitter that information, which may be unwelcome.

Astral mediumship is the type of mediumship I practice, but I no longer practice it professionally, and I no longer do it by request. If I am online, and I feel drawn to someone who is asking for a medium reading, I will find the departed first, and if it's going to be a pleasant reading for the sitter, then I offer it. Otherwise, I say nothing at all and move on. This is the only way I have found to overcome the drawbacks of having to report unfavorable information.

Tools of Mediumship

Automatic Writing

Some mediums, especially channeling mediums, use a pad of paper and a pen rather than speaking. As they go into a trance, they begin to make squiggly lines on the paper. Eventually, they begin to write words and phrases. The writing is a result of the spirit controlling their hand. So, the words that are written on the page form a message the spirit is trying to speak.

The medium may ask the spirit questions, or the sitter may ask the medium questions while he or she continues with the automatic writing. It's the same principle as tarot. Only in tarot, The Divine is controlling the psychic's hands while he or she shuffles and deals the cards.

You don't see automatic writing a great deal these days. However, it's very useful in some settings. It's used mostly during seances or when a person is trying to contact whatever spirit might be present in a room at the time.

You may also see it used (or use it yourself) during a paranormal investigation or while ghost hunting in a supposed haunted house. But it's not used for personal client -based sessions too much. It can be too impersonal. The medium typically shows no empathy or connection with the sitter while he or she is in the trance, and the communications can be fragmented. That's why most client-based mediumship is done through spiritual mediumship. There's more of a personal touch.

Talking Boards

Talking boards have been around since at least 1100 AD. They were used during the Song Dynasty in China and called, "fuji" (which means "planchette writing"). They were a tool of automatic writing, and were used as a

central practice of the Quanzhen School (a form of Tao-
ism). It is said that many of the writings of the Daozang
(a Taoist bible) are works of automatic planchette writing. It is also believed that planchette writing was used in
ancient India, Greece, Rome, as well as medieval Europe.

However, the more popular talking board known as the
Ouija board began in 1890, when its inventor, Elijah
Bond patented it as a board game. Spiritualists in America had already been using talking boards a great deal before this, but the Ouija board is what we are most familiar
with today.

The name "Ouija" means nothing. It is reported that
Elijah Bond and his partners asked the board what its
name was, and it spelled out, o-u-i-j-a, so that's what they
called their talking board.

You probably know what a talking board looks like:
There is the board with the letters of the alphabet on it;
below that are the numbers 0-9. In the upper left-hand
corner is the word, yes, and in the upper right-hand corner
is the word, no. Below the numbers at the bottom of the
board is the word, goodbye.

There is planchette, a small piece of plastic or wood
with a hole cut out of the middle to view the letters and
numbers, and it is often shaped like a teardrop, with the
narrow end used as a kind-of pointer.

When used solo, the medium puts his or her fingertips
on the planchette and enter a trance. They will then begin
to move the planchette around the board as they feel
"pushed" to move it, or they will move it in the direction
that feels less resistive. Ironically, after a bit of move-

ment, telepathy with the entity may break through and make the board unnecessary for communication.

Of course, it is more common that one or two other persons will put their fingertips on the planchette along with the medium, and the medium will ask the questions they want the spirit entity to answer.

Though the Ouija board is still a popular board game manufactured by Hasbro©, there is a widespread fear of Ouija boards that comes primarily from urban legends. Some people believe talking boards are portals for demonic spirits, and once you let a demon through, there's no getting it back from whence it came. Thus, it is believed you can become demon possessed while using the Ouija board. Then there are the reports of the planchette flying off the board and attacking people. Again, this has more to do with Hollywood notions of Ouija boards being evil than any reality associated with them.

Talking boards are intended as an aid for automatic writing. They always have been. There's really nothing more to them than that. But even the Ouija board game feeds the fear of talking boards (no doubt for marketing purposes) by including in the box the following rules:

Never use the Ouija board if you think it's just a game.

Never use the Ouija board alone.

Never use the Ouija board in a cemetery.

Never leave the planchette on the Ouija board when you aren't using it.

Never forget to say Goodbye to the Ouija spirits.

If you choose to use a talking board (Ouija or some other manufacturer or artist's version), don't be afraid of it. That will surely render it useless to you as a tool. Instead, see it for what it is, a board and planchette. You the medium have all the power, and you choose if it's the tool for you or not.

Black Mirrors

Black mirrors are made from a piece of glass, like the glass from a picture frame that has been painted black on one side. This forms a darkened mirror that can then be used like a window by mediums to see spirits on the astral plane.

The most popular story using a mirror for mediumship is in the Grimm Brothers fairytale, *Snow White*. If you remember, the wicked stepmother gazes into a mirror and recites: *Looking-glass upon the wall, who's the fairest of them all?* And a spirit comes into view in the mirror and routinely tells her that she is the most beautiful in the land—that is until Snow White shows up.

Typically, a medium will light candles in front of a black mirror and stare into it to see the spirits that have crossed over to the other side. This technique is called, scrying.

In fact, a medium may use scrying in conjunction with a talking board. In that case, the black mirror helps the medium focus their clairvoyance, while the board aids with automatic writing.

However, like the Ouija board, some people feel a black mirror can allow evil entities to enter a room and cause spiritual or physical harm, but again, a black mirror is just a tool. Unless it's used, it just hangs there like any other mirror.

If you're interested in using a black mirror, just obtain one or make one yourself. Set it on a table and light a candle beside it or in front of it. Then relax and stare into it. As you allow yourself to enter a trance, you will begin to see images. Are the images in the mirror or does the mirror simply allow you to focus your psychic sight inward? Only you can decide that, but if you're a medium, it can be a tool worth trying.

Becoming a Medium

The medium-type is a sensitive and caring individual. Often, they're empathic, meaning they can feel the grief and pain of others, and so they naturally want to help people reconnect with their loved ones. However, that doesn't mean that mediums are emotional pushovers.

Mediums must be very capable of grounding and shielding, or they won't last very long as mediums. For that reason, at times, mediums can seem aloof or cold, but once they are with a client, they are all in, and the emotional connection they make with the departed and the sitter is very personal and warm.

For that reason, perhaps the number one requirement for being a medium is wanting to be one in the first place. There is a significant emotional taxing that occurs. It may be difficult to deal with the grieving clients who have lost a loved one. A client may demand specific answers when the clairvoyance you are experiencing is more cloudy than clear. Or the sitter's expectations may be unreasonable in that they want to hear something from the departed that the departed simply is not willing to communicate.

The stress of these factors can cause empathic burnout over time, and any prospective medium should plan on taking sabbaticals from practicing the art as necessary. They may find that practicing a second psychic art allows for a natural break from mediumship when it is needed.

However, if one wants to be a medium or feels called to be one, they should practice. It's that simple. They should try it out and decide if it's for them.

It's very easy to find psychic reading groups online with loads of people wanting medium readings. Find one and dive in. Look at the photo of the deceased that is posted, and relate the impressions of what you are getting from it. You may find you have quite the knack.

After all, there is no one best way to learn how to be a medium. Ultimately, you must teach yourself, because only you know what makes you feel a connection, and you can only figure that out through trial and error.

That said, for those who feel a strong connection with spirits, being a medium may be something they simply have to do in order to feel complete. The only way to know that is to try it. You can also watch some professional television personalities who give medium readings. You can find them quite easily on YouTube. See how they work and try to imitate that if it feels like something you can incorporate.

If you are in an area where there is a Spiritualist church, you might attend their services and see how the mediums work. There are not a lot of Spiritualist churches around like there were in the 1800's, but there are still some.

Nevertheless, the rise of Facebook groups that feature psychic readings, has meant that a sitter can easily find a medium these days via the computer. By the same token, you can easily be that medium if you want to be. Try it on for size and see if it's a fit.

Chapter 9

The Witch

———— • ————

In Salem Village, they started by arresting the old women first. Tituba, the slave, was arrested, but there were many others. It was the summer of 1692 in Massachusetts, and though Betty Parris and her friends were accusing anyone they didn't like, they never accused you. You were the little girl who always sung, smiled, and helped clean the church after services, and Betty thought of you like a sister, so they never pointed a finger at you.

Two days before Betty and Abigail Williams started having their fits, two days before it was said that witches were in the village afflicting them, while you were in the barn cleaning the stalls, your black cat and the billy goat came and spoke to you.

You heard them in your mind, even though they just stood there staring. They told you to go, in two days, under the full moon, to the edge of the forest where the Goddess would be waiting for you, and so you did.

You snuck out of your bed from the loft and walked to the forest in your nightgown in the light of the moon. And there by a big oak tree where you had once carved your initials, a beautiful woman in a sheer black dress stood waiting. She reached out her hand, and you took it, and you walked with her deeper into the trees until you stopped in a clearing by a creek.

The woman took a long dagger and handed it to you. It was your father's dagger, and you wondered how she got it. You want to ask, but she spoke to you telling you to draw a circle on the ground with the dagger and to stand in the middle of it. And so, you did.

Then she told you, "Whatever you bid me do, I shall do it for you. For the time of sorrow has come. But one day, this very place will be for you and your kind. And I will keep you safe until then. If you will come here on the nights like this, draw a circle with this knife, stand in it and speak honestly to me of your desires, then I will do whatever you ask."

There was a radiant warmth in the circle, and your body felt light enough to rise into the air. You turned to ask if she was God, but when you did, she faded like a mist, and her mist was absorbed by the trees, and it flowed into the creek, and fell into the leaves on the ground. Then she disappeared, but you still felt her presence, like she hadn't gone at all, like she'd become everywhere and in everything.

When they hung Miss Bridget by her neck, you were there to see it, the whole town was. She was the first of many, and you always secretly admired Bridget Bishop. She owned a tavern and was outspoken among the men in town. The men of the town didn't like that, but you knew she wasn't like you. And you were pretty sure who they were really looking for was, in fact, you.

———————

The first thing you must understand about witchcraft is that it didn't begin in the seventeenth century in Salem, Massachusetts. Witchcraft is the oldest form of human spiritual practice there is. Prehistoric art shows what seems to be magical ceremonies related to hunting, and what could even be religious rituals with people dancing in animal costumes.

All societies and civilizations have their witches, and the practice of witchcraft goes back so far there's really no telling when it began. At least, that is, if witchcraft is defined broadly.

A broad definition of witchcraft is any use of mental intention and ritual to bring about an altered reality in the physical world. (That's called magick.) Usually, but not always, the magick of witchcraft is aided by invoking the help of a deity, a god, of some kind.

But the definition of witchcraft is even more broad if one includes in it any form of divination, healing, conjuring, or mediumship. Anyone who engages in any of those activities is likely to be called a witch by the major religions of the world.

And if that's the case, one soon realizes that witchcraft is imbedded in all our lives to some degree. Any kind of spellcasting is clearly witchcraft. So, blowing out candles on a birthday cake while closing your eyes and making a wish is, in fact, witchcraft. Throwing salt over your shoulder for protection is a spell, and so it too is witch-craft.

Even in the religious practices that you find in many churches on any given Sunday, involve what is technical-ly spell work (e.g., the transubstantiation of bread and wine into the body and blood of Christ during the Mass). And yet, regular religious practices performed in a tem-ple, mosque, or church, are not called witchcraft. But why?

The reason is that witches (as opposed to priests, min-isters, rabbis, and imams) are deliberately outside of the mainstream. Witches are not anti-social per se, but they are by nature countercultural. It's for that reason that Je-sus was accused of being a sorcerer (Matthew 12:24). He was performing miracles and controlling demons, but he was doing it outside of the authority of the temple, thus he was considered by the Jews to be a witch.

Personally, I grew up in the Pentecostal form of Chris-tianity. In the church I attended as a boy, I saw all forms of miracle working. I saw dancing around "in the spirit." I saw people fall on the ground and shake. I saw people faint when the pastor laid his hands on them. I heard peo-ple crying out in tongues (speaking in tongues), and prophecies were given to individuals all the time. To be honest, I've seen Voodoo ceremonies that were more con-servative. None of this, however, is considered witchcraft, because it is all done within the confines of a socially-sanctioned religion. Witches are not socially sanctioned; they never have been, never will be.

That said, if one stands apart from all of it, if one looks at it all from the outside, it's all the practice of magick. Socially acceptable magick is called religion. Socially unacceptable magick is called witchcraft.

So, where do you stand? Are you a witch? Let's move on, and perhaps you'll find out. There are three main categories of witches today. The solitary witch, the Wiccan, and the sorcerer. We'll examine each below.

The Solitary Witch

The solitary witch practices alone. They may be male or female. It is often thought that witches are primarily female, but even a cursory examination of the craft reveals as many men involved in witchcraft throughout history as women. For instance, 30 of the 130 arrested during the Salem witch trials were men. Shamanism (an early witchcraft of native peoples throughout the world) is traditionally male, and it was a man who started the religion of Wicca, and a man who brought Wicca to the United States. So, it's certainly an equal opportunity craft.

Sometimes men are called warlocks rather than witches, and sometimes a women sorcerer is called a sorceress, but these are older terms which aren't used much anymore. Now, a witch is anyone who practices witchcraft, and a sorcerer is anyone who practices sorcery.

The solitary witch may be the purest form of a witch. I say that because such a person is completely self-motivated to be a witch; they typically invent their own systems and spells, and they possess a unique relationship with their own revelation of the Divine. The deity they worship and invoke in magick is often known only to them.

So, the solitary witch is very much an individualist. They don't play well with others when it comes to magick, and they prefer to stand out as unique creations in the world. They aren't necessarily anti-social, in fact they may be very committed to social causes, environmental protection, or animal welfare, but people, and especially crowds, tend to drain them. A long walk at midnight may be preferred to dancing the night away in a club. Visiting an isolated beach in the moonlight may be preferable to a spring break in Miami.

Also, the solitary witch is more likely to have descended from a line of witches, and thus feel drawn into the craft. This lineage may be genetic. That is, their mother may have been a witch, their grandmother, great grandmother, etc. But more often it is a spiritual lineage from previous lives. That is, they were a witch in their immediate past life, and may have been one in several lives before that. These lives may have a very powerful influence on them. Thus, the lineage can be genetic or spiritual.

The bottom line is that the solitary witch is someone who wants to be left alone with their magick, their god, and the spirits they surround themselves with. They may be very secretive about their practices, and for that reason you may never know that such a person is a witch.

The real danger is when the solitary witch doesn't know that they are a witch. They aren't around other witches, so no one notices the potential in them, and thus no one tells them about it. When a person is a witch unknown to themselves, their natural gift of turning intent into magick can go unchecked.

In theory, if a witch does not come to understand that he or she is a witch, their thoughts and the power of their natural witchcraft may unwittingly alter their world for the good or for the bad. In other words, it's out of control.

It's an age-old notion that if you don't want something bad to happen you shouldn't mention it. Or that it's wrong to think evil about someone, lest you cause it to happen to them. On the other hand, positive thinking is greatly valued and many believe it can result in good fortune. All of this comes from the idea that one can be practicing witchcraft and not know it. In the case of the solitary witch who doesn't know they are a witch, this effect can be amplified.

Sometimes, if a person feels witchcraft is bad or against their religion, they may suppress their magical nature. But it comes out anyway, eventually. So, it is far better to embrace it, learn it, systematize it, and even keep a journal of it. Such journal is often called a *grimoire* (pronounced, *grim-wah* or *grim-war*, your choice). In this way, the solitary witch, can come to have better control over the circumstances that shape the destiny of their life, and maybe the lives of others.

So, are you a solitary witch? There is no definitive test for this, but there are five clues that can indicate it.

Are you a solitary witch?

1. Do you feel attracted to witchcraft? The very first clue one is a witch is if they feel a desire to be a witch.

That desire comes from somewhere, and more likely than not, it comes from a genetic or past-life lineage.

2. Do you suspect your thoughts (at any time) have influenced your environment? Have you ever wished for something and then it came true? This could be something good or bad; it doesn't matter. Either way, it shows a latent ability for witchcraft.

3. Do you feel spiritual but not religious? You may even hate religion and yet feel very close to God. You may suspect that God is not what they are talking about in your church, but rather something you feel you uniquely understand.

4. Do you feel a kinship to animals. This is because witches have a power that is attractive to animal minds, and because spirits like to be around witches, they may possess animals in order to be physically around the witch. This kind of animal is called a *familiar*. The spiritual attraction of the familiar goes both ways. The animal loves the witch, and the witch loves the animal.

5. Do you have an astrological sun sign or a rising sign, that is in Scorpio, Pisces, or Cancer? Though one can have these signs and not be a witch, or vice versa, it's just another supporting clue. The water signs are more conducive to witchcraft.

If any one of these is true of you, you may be a solitary witch. If they are all true, you are definitely a witch.

The Wiccan

Wicca is the organized religion of witches. It's possible to be a solitary witch and practice Wicca, but Wicca is more often a communal experience. It's made up of covens, which are groups of like-minded witches who meet at regular intervals to perform specific pagan rites through the practice of witchcraft.

A coven is usually headed by a high priest or priestess, and new members must be initiated and work their way up through the ranks to become full-fledged witches. The general hierarchy is made up of four degrees starting with the initiate and ending with the priest or priestess, but each coven has their own specific hierarchy.

Wicca focuses on a reverence for nature and the worship of a dual deity called the God and Goddess. Just who the God and Goddess are, and which one is worshiped, can vary from coven to coven, but usually it's some form of what they call the Moon Goddess and the Horned God.

Unlike other organized religions, Wicca has no central authority that is recognized by all. There is, however, an organization which is Wicca's largest organization called the Coven of the Goddess. It was formed in 1975 as a diverse group of covens that wanted to secure the legal protections and benefits of an official church. They formed the Covenant of the Goddess (CoG), which is incorporated in the State of California and recognized by the Internal Revenue Service.

But covens in Wicca are essentially autonomous from one another. And like any religion, Wicca has several denominations, which they call *traditions* (e.g., Gardnerian Wicca, Dianic Wicca, Celtic Wicca, etc.). That said, there are still things that are common to all Wiccans:

Standard Wiccan Beliefs

- Wiccans are pagan witches.

- The pentagram is the symbol for the Wiccan religion.

- Wiccans believe the Divine is found primarily through nature.

- Wiccans hold two basic moral principles:

  * What you put out in actions or magick, you get back three-fold (the Three-fold Principle).

  * So long as what you do harms no one, do whatever you want (the Wiccan Rede).

- Wiccans celebrate the following festivals, called *sabbats*, as a means of attunement to the seasonal rhythms of Nature. These are:

  * January 31 (February Eve)

  * March 21 (Spring Equinox)

  * April 30 (May Eve)

  * June 22 (Summer Solstice)

  * July 31 (Lammas)

  * September 21 (Autumn Equinox)

  * October 31 (Hallows)

  * December 21 (Winter Solstice)

Wiccan History

In 1939, Gerald Gardner, a 52-year-old Englishman from Dorset, began the formation of Wicca after studying witchcraft from an array of sources. Gardner was born in, Lancashire, England, but lived mostly abroad.

As an adult, in British Malaysia, he worked in a civil service capacity, but on his own time, he developed an interest in the magical practices of the native peoples of that area. After his retirement in 1936, he returned to England and joined an occult group, the Rosicrucian Order Crotona Fellowship. While with them, he encountered the New Forest coven and was initiated into it 1939.

It was from that experience that he formed Gardnerian tradition of Wicca. Essentially, he combined the New Forest coven's rituals with ideas borrowed from Freemasonry, ceremonial magic, and the writings of Aleister Crowley.

Later, Raymond Buckland, a student of Gerald Gardner, brought Gardnerian Wicca to the United States after immigrating in 1962. His book, *Buckland's Complete Book of Witchcraft*, written in 1986 is still considered the standard book of practice for many Wiccans.

Can you become a Wiccan? That all depends. It depends on whether you can find a coven and join it and whether you are willing to work through the coven's process for becoming a witch. You don't have to be born a witch to become a witch through Wicca. Wicca is a religion. Thus, joining a Wiccan coven and participating in the rites and rituals, and doing the work of progressing through the levels, makes you a witch.

One advantage to Wiccan practice is that one enjoys the social support of other witches, and it can be said that the communal practice of witchcraft produces faster and stronger results than merely practicing alone. Not to mention, it's an effective way to make like-minded friends and have people to be with when celebrating the sabbats.

The Sorcerer

Sometimes the words *sorcery* and *witchcraft* are used interchangeably, but there is a distinct difference between a sorcerer and a classical witch. Here are the three major differences:

1. Sorcerers conjure.

A sorcerer typically employs the use of other spirits to help him or her with their magical practice. That is why they have a reputation for *conjuring*.

Conjuring is calling up spirits from the astral plane to give you advice, predict the future, accomplish some task, influence other people, or simply to commune with. These spirits can be any kind of spirit but usually they are a form of a demon or daemon.

A *demon* is any malevolent spirit that does, or is used to do, bad things. For instance, a regular witch may put a curse on someone using his or her own intention and spell work, a sorcerer would summon a demon and send it to that person to accomplish the curse.

A daemon (pronounced *day-mon*), on the other hand, is a helper spirit. They typically guard people, ward off demons and other troublesome spirits, and warn the sorcerer of danger. Statues are made of daemons in the form of gargoyles on buildings, or even in the form of a jack-olantern on Halloween. They could easily be considered spirit guides or guardian angels by persons other than sorcerers.

So, while many other witches may be doing spells to protect against demons, the sorcerer is often doing rituals to summon them.

Another form of conjuring is called *necromancy*. Necromancy means casting a spell or using a demon to call up the dead to gain information from them, but it's not the same thing as mediumship.

The sorcerer does not act as a medium between a departed loved one and a family member or friend. Rather, the sorcerer forces up a dead person's spirit to gain information about the past, present, or future, or to use them to gain knowledge about the astral realm.

2. Sorcerers practice dark magick.

No doubt, you have heard the terms white magick and black magick. White magic is witchcraft done to help or heal. Black magick is witchcraft done to harm or curse. But then there is dark magick.

Dark magick is what sorcerers practice. Dark magick is primarily selfish. It is witchcraft that focuses primarily on spells for money, spells to control others' actions, spells to favor one's own situation, and sometimes even to harm someone for revenge or justice. It can be spells to increase one's influence in the world, or divination done to gain advantage over a competitor.

These are examples of dark magick. The spells are not evil, per se; not like black magick, but neither is it benevolent or altruistic. It's not light, like a blessing on a new-born, or a healing incantation, a love potion, or a fertility spell. Dark magick is only for the benefit of the magician performing the spell.

So, not surprisingly, sorcerers typically do not enjoy a positive reputation. Sorcerers, however, would consider themselves witches who are simply keeping it real. They aren't evil, but they aren't good. They are simply self-serving.

3. Sorcerers are made not born.

Sorcerers are not natural witches, though a natural witch could be a sorcerer. Sorcery is a learned craft through the continuous study of the occult as well as trial and error application of techniques used to summon spirits who carry out the desired magick.

For this reason, sorcerers tend to be serious academics of the occult. They study diligently and tend to have lots of books and manuals, and grimoires. And so, they have a reputation for wisdom and spiritual depth.

But anyone can be a sorcerer if they have the desire to be. All the natural talent that comes with being born a witch may help one be a more effective sorcerer, but all that is really needed is a desire to learn the art. The normal psychic powers that all people possess are more than enough to further the sorcerer along his or her path. Thus, it is said a sorcerer is made, whereas a witch is born.

So, how does one know what kind of witch they are? How do they know what path to follow? The answer is simple. One need only examine themselves honestly.

Are you more of an individual player, or do you prefer a community? If you're more individual in nature, then you should pursue solitary witchcraft. If you like being in a group of likeminded people, search out a Wiccan coven to join, or start one of your own. Reach out and get involved.

Maybe you feel you weren't really born to be a witch but you're intellectually into the occult and you love the idea of magick to increase your chances of a good life on earth; sorcery could be just the ticket, especially if you're attracted to the darker side of things and the creatures that inhabit the astral plane. In the end, it's all about honest self-evaluation.

Conclusion

In the end, there are two ways a person can live their life. They can live it believing the physical world is all there is. When it's over, they blink out of existence as if they were never here. Or, they can live in the truth that they are a spiritual being incarnated for a brief time in the physical world and headed for greater destinies hereafter.

If we try to live like physical people only, we soon find there's no real purpose in life. Everything is born, it thrives for a time, it declines, and it dies, and that cycle seems to repeat forever. If we could be completely ignorant of our spiritual nature, if like the animals we had no concept of our impending demise, then we could tolerate that purely physical existence.

But we do know of our spiritual nature, and we are aware of our psychic self. The mind is both psychological and parapsychological, and to neglect the latter half of it means failing to fully develop as human beings, and mentally that becomes intolerable over time.

So, I implore you to dive in to your psychic self. Try to understand what you really are, what God really is, and that your mind is completely independent of your body. Apply the psychic skills of centering, grounding, and shielding, and go discover your psychic art.

If you do these things, you can live this life at its highest level. You can transcend your physical self and find your integration with the Divine. I assure you that if you do, you will be happier and healthier than you've ever been, for life will have shown you the grand purpose for living it.

About the Author

Edward Gordon is a professional psychic and the host of *The Edward Gordon Hour* on YouTube. He's the owner/ admin of the largest and most popular psychic reading group on Facebook, *Free Psychic Readings*, and he maintains a private practice through his website at *EGspirit.me*. His previous works include, *Caretakers of Eternity*, *Vital Architecture and the New Design of Happiness*, *The Veridican Gospel of Jesus Christ,* and *Tarot: The Dark Art*. He is currently working on his next book and resides in the New Orleans area of the United States with his wife, three dogs and two cats.

Edward's Website:

EGspirit.me

Edward's Facebook Page

https://www.facebook.com/edgordonrn

The Free Psychic Readings Facebook Group

https://www.facebook.com/groups/tarotanddreams

Edward's E-Mail:

Edward@EGspirit.me

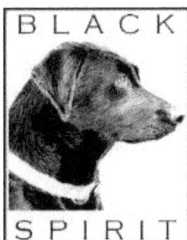

Black Spirit Publishing
P.O. Box 2428, PMB# 8443
Pensacola, FL 32513

www.ingramcontent.com/pod-product-compliance
Lightning Source LLC
LaVergne TN
LVHW051104080426

835508LV00019B/2061